D0068200

The
UNQUIET
Monk

THOMAS MERTON'S QUESTING FAITH

Michael W. Higgins

ORBIS BOOKS
www.orbisbooks.com

ORBIS BOOKS
Maryknoll, New York 10545
Second Priting, December 2015

Founded in 1970, Orbis Books endeavors to publish works that enlighten the mind, nourish the spirit, and challenge the conscience. The publishing arm of the Maryknoll Fathers and Brothers, Orbis seeks to explore the global dimensions of the Christian faith and mission, to invite dialogue with diverse cultures and religious traditions, and to serve the cause of reconciliation and peace. The books published reflect the views of their authors and do not represent the official position of the Maryknoll Society. To learn more about Maryknoll and Orbis Books, please visit our website at www.maryknollsociety.org.

Library of Congress Cataloging-in-Publication Data
Higgins, Michael W.
   The unquiet monk : Thomas Merton's questing faith / Michael W. Higgins.
     pages cm
    ISBN 978-1-62698-112-6 (pbk.)
    1. Merton, Thomas, 1915-1968. I. Title.
   BX4705.M542H55 2015
   271'.12502--dc23
   [B]

                                      2014033997

Contents

The writer is situated in his time;
every word he utters has reverberations.
As does his silence.

Jean-Paul Sartre

Introduction

THE UNQUIET MONK: Thomas Merton's Questing Faith is the result of many labours, a testament to the perduring interest in and relevance of Thomas Merton, monk, poet and critic, and a timely contribution to understanding this endlessly fascinating, complex and multivalent genius on the very cusp of the centenary of his birth in the south of France.

A monk who spoke to the world from the cloisters of his Kentucky home, Thomas Merton is truly one of the most remarkable figures of our time. Journalist, photographer, novelist, poet, social and political critic, calligrapher, essayist, priest. He addressed himself to the crises of modern humanity from the confines of a medieval establishment. Dorothy Day, Eldridge Cleaver, Boris Pasternak, Lenny Bruce, Jacques Maritain—the names of those who knew and admired him are legion. The man of poverty bequeathed to his adopted nation, America, a conscience, and to the world a vision of sanity and generosity.

To help identify the singularity of Merton's rich and sometimes controversial contributions to the intellectual and spiritual life of our time, we examine in this text his life, his poetry, his commitment to trenchant social criticism, his expansive and embracing religious imagination, his courageous dialogue with Eastern religions and his position as an icon of wholeness for a fractured, alienated postmodern generation. In the following chapters, Merton's life and work will unfold as viewed through the following prisms:

ERASMINIAN CRITIC

Following the tradition of the great Renaissance humanist, reformer and scourge of decadent monasticism, Merton denounced the inadequacies of an increasingly moribund institutional monasticism; he denounced the obsessive power politics of scheming prelates and abbots; he denounced the corporate mentality of Wall Street, the hegemony of U.S. mass culture, the contempt for genuine human freedom in American society; and he denounced the false superiority of Western civilization. Not surprisingly, there were many who in turn denounced him.

SWIFTIAN SATIRIST

The Adolf Eichmann affair—the famous 1960s kidnapping, trial and execution of the mastermind behind the implementation of the Final Solution (the destruction of European Jewry)—haunted Merton's moral imagination. In poem, essay and diary entry, often in bitterly ironic terms redolent of the savage satirical wit of the great Anglican divine Jonathan Swift, Merton excoriated the forensic and bankrupt sanity found in the Nazi manuals, edicts and propaganda. Their debasing of language allowed them to veil the monstrous truth of their evil, thereby contributing to the moral evacuation of humanity through word as well as through action. As a poet, Merton was determined to reclaim the word, cleanse it of its corruption, incarnate truth not falsehood in human discourse, narrative, metaphor and image.

CAMUSIAN REBEL

The celebrated Algerian-French existentialist and novelist Albert Camus was a symbol of moral and spiritual resistance for Merton, who wrote extensively about Camus' writing, his life, his witness to truth. Merton saw in Camus the consummate rebel, the writer who refused alienation, and he saw the key to shattering the allure and hold of alienation in contemplation. Merton's writings on the various dimensions of contemplation—no longer seen as the exclusive preserve of consecrated religious and cloistered monastics—contributed immensely to his popularity among Catholics and non-Catholics.

CISTERCIAN PROPHET

Merton's understanding of contemplation—sophisticated, highly nuanced, historically flavoured and spiritually expansive—and his exercise of the role of prophecy combined to guarantee his continued reputation as a monk open to the world, a critic of Catholicism's institutional inadequacy, and an astute and rigorous judge of the world's political, social and philosophical pathologies of the spirit.

BLAKEAN VISIONARY

Merton saw the only antidote to Western society's enthrallment by Reason and Abstraction, the tyranny of Logic, and the life-constricting Sanity that has no place for Feeling, Imagination and Vision in the wisdom poetics and visual artistry of the heterodox Christian genius William Blake.

What follows is an orderly exploration of the life and thought of Merton understood in the context of his multivalent probes of the human spirit: the poet, the contemplative, the political and social critic, the spiritual visionary and the pilgrim to the East.

In addition to Merton's own voice, you will hear from many of his friends, fellow monks, biographers and scholars of his thought. The extensive quotations that appear throughout the text are the result of oral interviews with the author, both onsite and studio-generated, much of which has not previously been published.

Thomas Merton, the Unquiet Monk, never ceased to engage and provoke. It is no different now, a centenary since his birth in a small town in the French Pyrenees.

1

Merton:
The Biography

MERTON WAS A perpetual pilgrim: a pilgrim of the mind, the imagination, and the spirit. He was even born en route: his parents, itinerant artists, caught up in the turmoil of an embattled France. He wrote of his birth:

> On the last day of January 1915, under the sign of the Water-Bearer, in the year of a great war, and down in the shadow of some French mountains on the borders of Spain, I came into the world. . . . I inherited from my father his way of looking at things and some of his integrity, and from my mother, some of her dissatisfaction with the mess the world was in, and some of her versatility. From both I got capacities for work and vision and enjoyment and expression that ought to have made me some kind of King, if the standards the world lives by were the real ones. Not that we ever had any money: but any fool knows that you don't need money to get enjoyment out of life.
>
> If what most people take for granted were really true—if all you needed to be happy was to grab everything and see everything and investigate every experience and then talk about it, I should have been a very happy person, a spiritual millionaire, from the cradle even until now.
>
> If happiness were merely a matter of natural gifts, I would

never have entered a Trappist monastery when I came to the age of a man.

Merton wrote these lines as the opening to his highly successful autobiography, *The Seven Storey Mountain*. The work was published in 1948 while the author was but 33 years of age. He had entered the Trappist monastery of Our Lady of Gethsemani in the hills of Kentucky seven years previously, on December 10, 1941. For years, Merton longed to know both where he was and, perhaps more importantly, *who* he was.

John Howard Griffin, writer, journalist, and official biographer of Thomas Merton until his own final serious illness and then death in 1980, has this to say of Merton's early years:

Tom was born in Prades on the 31st of January, 1915, at 9:30 at night. And by the end of the first year he was baptized, even though this was probably Owen's doing, the father's doing, because the mother didn't want any spurious religious influences brought to bear until he was of an age to decide for himself.

She's been considered rather coldly by some people who know her only through Thomas Merton's writings. To my mind she had, as her diaries show, a profound love and a profound concern for that child, and as I say, a certain discomfort because he was not doing what the books said that an 18-month-old or a two-year-old child should be doing. He was a remarkably rapid learner but he didn't care anything about toys; he cared about images, he cared about the music that his father played—his father was an accomplished pianist—and he very quickly learned words. As the war approached, they decided to come to America.

They came to America; Owen was in such an anguish over the war that he couldn't paint so he took a job as a landscape gardener and he also played the piano in the local theatre, until one day, in 1921 it was, when Tom was 6 years old—and probably the first big shattering shock of his life—his mother disappeared and no one really let him know anything about it. But his dad handed him a letter—he could by then read very, very well—it was a letter that his mother had written; she was hospitalized in Bellevue Hospital for cancer of the stomach and she was terminal, and she had kept this from him. She believed that nothing unpleasant or morbid should be known by children. His reaction to that note, he said, was a reaction not of childish grief, but of profound adult sorrow and misery in the sense, as he said, [that] "My mother was informing me by mail that she was about to die and would never see me again."

After his mother's death, Merton spent some time with his beloved grandparents, Pop and Bonnemaman. From his grandfather, particularly, he learned of the somewhat odious associations affixed to being Catholic.

My grandparents were like most other Americans: they were Protestants. But you could never find out precisely what kind of Protestants they were. I, their own grandson, was never able to ascertain. They put money in the little envelopes that came to them from Zion Church, but they never went near the place itself, and they also contributed to the Salvation Army and a lot of other things; so you couldn't tell what they were by the places which they helped to support.

On the whole, the general attitude around that house was the more or less inarticulate assumption that all religions were more or less praiseworthy on purely natural or social grounds. In any decent suburb of a big city you'd expect to run across some kind of a church once in a while; it was part of the scenery, like the High School, and the YMCA, and the big whale-back roof, and water tank of the movie theater.

The only exceptions to this general acceptability of religions were the Jews and the Catholics. Who would want to be a Jew? But then, that was a matter of race more than of religion.

The Jews were Jews but they couldn't very well help it. But as for the Catholics, it seemed in Pop's mind that there was a certain sinister note of malice connected with the profession of anything like the Catholic faith. The Catholic Church was the only one against which I've ever heard him speak with any definite bitterness or animosity.

At the age of ten, the young Merton went with his father back to his homeland; his younger brother, John-Paul, his only sibling, remained behind with his grandparents. This French period, however, was to be short-lived. He endured a brief and quite miserable time at the Lycée Ingres in Montauban, which, if anything, toughened him for the English public schools to which he was to be sent at the age of thirteen. Within two years of his return to England, his father died, and Thomas was entrusted to the care of a guardian—his godfather and a close friend of his father's, a Harley Street specialist by the name of Tom. The young Merton was now on the threshold of his rebellious stage.

John Howard Griffin summarizes the rollercoaster ride of the emerging Merton:

He had a tremendous kind of effervescence that made him want to scandalize everybody, and he was leading as wild a life as he knew how to lead, and he took a trip in the summers: he would usually take off and go to Europe, and he would hitchhike, at a time when I suppose there had been very little hitchhiking in history, into France, into Italy, through Alsace. He was a man who had no religious background whatsoever besides having been baptized when he was one year old. He began to be deeply attracted to certain aspects of the Catholic faith, largely through his love of art. He fell in love and became passionately in love with the frescoes in the churches; he would try to visit these at times when nobody would be there; if there was sign of anybody he would flee from the church. He also had at that time a strange kind of a vision, and this was one night in Italy when he was getting ready to sleep: he never knew what it was, but he had an immense impression of his father's presence, and this again, contrasted to the kind of life that he was trying to lead, which was a life entirely of the senses and the exploration of the senses; it was a fairly shattering experience for him.

In 1933, Merton entered Clare College, Cambridge, on a scholarship. It proved, however, uncongenial to his temperament. Within a year, he left for New York and Columbia University. He was much happier here, and he flourished in the social, political and literary atmosphere of this far from sylvan setting. Literary activities became a major feature of his life, and he assumed editorial positions with various campus publications. After his undergraduate work was completed, he began work on his MA thesis, *Nature and Art in William Blake.* The year before he completed his thesis, 1938, he converted to Roman Catholicism.

William Nicholls, an Anglican priest, fellow graduate of Clare College, and one-time chair of the Department of Religious Studies at the University of British Columbia, sees Merton's quest for identity taking shape very early and remaining a driving factor for many years, both prior to and in the monastery itself:

Coming from a mixed family—his father was a New Zealander, and his mother American—and living during his childhood and youth in three different countries, he found himself at least a bit out of place everywhere, and he only gradually settled on being an American, after he had left Cambridge in disgust and self-disgust in November 1934. That part of his struggle for identity only ended, or its ending was only formally acknowledged, when he became an American citizen in 1951. Meanwhile, another struggle for identity at the level of religion had been in progress for an even longer period.

In the second half of *The Seven Storey Mountain*, Thomas Merton tells the story of his *efforts* to find a religious identity for himself. As a boy he had envied others the security of their own identification with a traditional religion. His schooling in England and its association with the Church of England did nothing to give him what he felt he lacked. A decisive step was taken with his conversion to Catholicism in November 1938. Just joining the Roman Catholic Church was not enough to satisfy Merton's longing for an identity. He wanted to throw himself into this new role as completely as he could, to efface all traces of any other religious identity. He became a frequent communicant, began to pray and read books on prayer, he thought of the priesthood, and even of entering a monastery, first as a Franciscan, and then more decisively as a Cistercian.

After his reception into the Roman Church, Merton agonized over his future as a Catholic and determined to pursue a course of action that would involve him directly in the life of his Church. Attracted by the work of a titanesque Russian émigré, the Baroness Catherine de Hueck, Merton tried his hand at apostolic labour in Harlem, New York, but it was not what he needed. He then thought of his future in terms of a vocation as a teacher, and later as a Franciscan friar, but to no avail. It would be as a monk of the Cistercians of the Strict Observance, more commonly known as Trappists, that Merton would realize his destiny.

Prior to going on a retreat to Gethsemani—his first—to spend Holy Week, Merton read the entry on the Trappists in the *Catholic Encyclopedia* and was transfixed by what he read. He marvelled at their freedom, their joy in silence and solitude, their delight in working with their hands, their freedom from the rat race of contemporary living. They were masters in their own house: they built their own habitations, fed themselves, constructed their own furniture, made their own coarse clothing, happily repudiated the allurements of the flesh—the seductions proffered by the world, seductions grounded in falsity and illusory freedom and happiness. What he read fed his romantic imagination and persuaded him that these simple, poor and primitive men were the last and the least of Christ's poor and rejected, and that in this status was their salvation and their joy. And he would have some of that.

Donald Grayston, an Anglican priest, is the author of *Thomas Merton's Rewritings: The Five Versions of Seeds and New Seeds of Contemplation* and of *Thomas Merton: The Development of a Spiritual Theologian*. He observes of Merton's alienation from his century some important features of his embryonic piety and vocation:

> Merton found himself alienated from his own century. He called it, you know, a disgusting century, full of poison gas and atomic bombs. Well you really only . . . most people really only have two choices: to live in your century, to live in the time that you are born in, and make the best of it, or suicide. In other words, remove yourself from your century. Well, Merton committed a certain clever kind of suicide: he died to the world; in fact, he uses metaphors of suicide in *The Seven Storey Mountain* and says, talks about, you know, killing his former life and so on. But it wasn't physical suicide; what it was was a kind of time travel.
>
> There's an interesting bit in *The Man in the Sycamore Tree*, an early memoir/biography by his Columbia University friend Ed Rice, where Rice says that the way of life at Gethsemani when Merton went there in 1940 was essentially the Trappist regime of 17th-century France unchanged, right down to the big straw

hats that the monks wore, and the horse-drawn wagons, and so on; you could have gone right back to La Trappe in France and that's what it would have been like. So he travelled, but it was a travel in time by stages; first of all he became a Roman Catholic, and as we look at the Roman Catholic Church of the late '30s now, it really seems to be very much like the Roman Catholic Church of the 19th century—in other words, the full ultramontanism and the full triumphalism of the Roman Catholic Church in that broad period was still in full steam and it was putting out a clear story about, you know, in this naughty and chaotic world, if you want order in your life, become a Roman Catholic. It was a very, very good and convincing pitch, and it was what Merton needed and he accepted it and he joined up.

In his autobiography, Merton wrote of his welcome at Gethsemani:

I rang the bell at the gate. It let fall a dull, unresonant note inside the empty court.... Nobody came. I could hear somebody moving around inside the Gatehouse. I did not ring again. Presently, the window opened, and Brother Matthew looked out between the bars with his clear eyes and greying beard.... So Brother Matthew locked the gate behind me and I was enclosed in the four walls of my new freedom.

And it was appropriate that the beginning of freedom should be as it was. For I entered a garden that was dead and stripped and bare. The flowers that had been there last April were all gone. The sun was hidden behind low clouds and an icy wind was blowing over the gray grass and the concrete walks....

If I expected any grand welcome from Christ and His angels, I did not get it—not in the sensible order. The huge nave was like a tomb, and the building was as cold as ice. However, I did not mind. Nor was I upset by the fact that nothing special came into my head in the way of a prayer. I just knelt there more or less dumb, and listened to the saw down at the sawmill fill the air with long and strident complaints and the sound of labor.

Of Merton's early days in the monastery, his biographer John Howard Griffin says:

Nobody thought that he was going to stay with the Trappists; none of his friends thought that he was going to stay a Trappist. He's had too cushy a life, he's got too tremendous an intellect, and at that time the Trappists were considered an absolutely anti-intellectual order; they believed that a man entered the Trappists with a vocation to unite himself to God in solitude but living in community. The physical life was extremely hard. They lived under a rule of silence, and for a man like Merton, who was totally and utterly "unsilent," this seemed, you know, an impossibility. At that time they took no flesh food of any kind, the food consisted largely of boiled vegetables and fruits and cheese, maybe. It was an extremely ascetic life; they got up and began the day at 2 a.m., and it was a life of labour and prayer and silence, extraordinary silence. What communication had to be done was done with sign language, with Trappist sign language, and in fact if you needed to speak you had to go and get permission to speak; you were only allowed to speak to your novice master or to the abbot and that only with prior permission.

Grayston elaborates on these early days in the monastery:

So by becoming a Trappist he, as it were, went back and lived in the 17th century, but then he very soon saw that there was something more basic to the Trappists: Saint Bernard of Clairvaux and the Cistercians, and the contemplative stuff, so he went right back to that and became a kind of 12th-century primitive Cistercian; he was a kind of early Cistercian Father living in the 20th century, and then he got keen on the Desert Fathers, and the hermit life and that kind of thing, and so he went back another six centuries and lived as a hermit. In other words, he lived as a lot of people lived in the deserts of Egypt and Syria in the sixth century.

John Howard Griffin situates further the climate and the context:

> This was a cold place in the winter, and a very, very hot place in the summer. In those days there was no heat; they had one room where if you got terribly cold you could go in and warm up, but there was no heat in the sleeping rooms; they slept in dormitories, great dormitories that were partitioned off so that each monk had a little open cell, open at the floor and open at the top, and a curtain across, and in that was a cot which was a wooden platform with a straw-filled mattress and there was virtually nothing else.

Merton described the early years as a time in which he was swallowed up in obscurity, anonymity, a silent member of a family consecrated to silence. He lived according to the rule and regulations of Cistercian life, rose at 2:00 in the morning, jostled with other monks in the dark as he struggled to splash his face with water, settling into the choir adjacent to a monk with a cold, another singing off key, clustered together, awkward but in one flesh, one family, solitaries in community, all of a piece and in peace.

John Howard Griffin:

> Those years between his entry into the order and his spiritual development and his intellectual development were years of marvellous tranquility, in the sense that although they were very difficult, later, at the very end of his life, when they were talking about how some of these rigidities had been made more humane, Merton remarked, yes, but we were happy in those days, you know.

In the early years, Merton thought he had found both identity and peace, but soon a combination of the internal and external pressures began to disturb his newfound tranquility. William Nicholls describes Merton's early years at the abbey:

He adopted the new identity of Trappist monk with characteristic commitment and energy. The writings of his early years in the monastery display him as "super-monk"; nothing is neglected in his endeavour to become the perfect Trappist. No wonder he was permitted, indeed instructed, to write; he must have been the very model of what an aspiring young monk should be.

Under the influence, among other forces, of his own writings, scores, even hundreds of young men were drawn to the monastery. Being a Trappist, as he knew perfectly well, was a means to a greater end: in the first place by becoming a contemplative, and in the long run by becoming a saint. The notion that he should be a saint was not a new one; the idea had already come to him in his Columbia days.

One day, his Catholic convert friend and fellow poet Bob Lax turned around and asked him the question "What do you want to be, anyway?"

He could not say, "I want to be Thomas Merton the well-known writer of all those book reviews in the back pages of the *New York Times Book Review*, or Thomas Merton the assistant instructor of freshman English at the New Life Social Institute for Progress and Culture," so he put this thing on the spiritual plane, where he knew it belonged, and said, "I don't know. I guess what I want is to be a good Catholic."

"What do you mean, you want to be a good Catholic?" Lax queried. The explanation he gave was lame enough, and expressed his confusion and betrayed how little he had really thought about it at all. Lax did not accept it. "What you should say," he told him, "what you should say is that you want to be a saint."

A saint. The thought struck Thomas Merton as bizarre. He asked Lax: "How do you expect me to become a saint?"

"By wanting to," said Lax simply.

The goal of becoming a saint, together with the notion that since this is God's will for humanity—the way to become a saint is to want to—runs through Merton's second major autobiographical work, *The Sign of Jonas*. But how concretely was it going to happen? The contemplative life suited Merton. The silence, the relative solitude, the simplicity of the life helped him to develop an innate capacity for meditation and contemplation. It soon turned out that things were not going to be as simple as that, however. When he entered Gethsemani, Merton tried to give up the idea of being a writer. His superiors thought otherwise. His ability to write was going to be helpful to the Order. Moreover, the abbot, Frederic Dunne, instructed him to go on writing poetry. Although you can write to order, and Merton did, you can't be a writer to somebody else's speci-fication. The results, he later came to acknowledge, were some terrible books, as with his hagiographies.

Of these various pressures, which in fact multiplied over the years, Merton wrote in his journal *Conjectures of a Guilty Bystander*:

Don R—, prominent in Italian Catholic Action and editor of a rather lavish magazine, writes a pleasant, breezy note, asking for an article on "The Holiness of the Church": just like that! People are now convinced that I secrete articles like perspira-tion. This is clearly more my fault than theirs, and something has to be done about it. And yet, if people were to really *read* me, they might not take it for granted that I could simply reach into the back of my mind for a dish of ready-to-serve Catholic answers about everything under the sun. It seems to me that one of the reasons why my writing appeals to many people is precisely that I am not so sure of myself and do not claim to have all the answers. In fact, I often wonder quite openly about these "answers," and about the habit of always having them ready. The best I can do is look for some of the questions.

Again and again, over the years Merton found himself assuming writing responsibilities that would easily deter a full-time writer, and this he was not, at least in the professional sense. He was a full-time monk, with diverse responsibilities to his community. But he was always the writer. In a relatively short period as a writer, about 28 years, in fact, Merton authored over 50 books, numberless articles, and a truly prolific correspondence that he conducted with both the humble and the great. Nicholls observes of Merton the writer that this feature of his life could not be denied.

He had to write for himself, not his superiors, including the censors, who sometimes usurped the role of literary critic. Later on we find him acknowledging that he was undoubtedly born to be a writer, although it might still be open to doubt whether he succeeded in becoming a monk. He began to feel the need of more silence and solitude still. The wish for more solitude led to a recurrent feeling that he was in the wrong order, that he ought to transfer to another, where he could live as a hermit, perhaps the Carthusians or maybe the Carmelites or the Camaldolese. Though he gradually learned to interpret it as a temptation, not a vocation, the feeling persisted for a number of years. *The Sign of Jonas* tells how he dealt with this problem. In the end it seemed to resolve itself with his appointment as novice master. Somehow his responsibility for others imposed on him an inner solitude which he found helpful to contemplation. Being alone did not have to mean being physically isolated. His paradoxical destiny, as he calls it, was to remain a Trappist and find the substance of solitude in the communal life.

In fact, Merton spoke to the novices of Gethsemani throughout his life, and fortunately the monks had the foresight to record these sessions. His 30-minute sessions on a wide range of topics—prayer, poets such as Rainer Maria Rilke, French novelists and scribes, monasticism, William Faulkner, John Cassian, a vast and eclectic canvas—were part lectures, part Socratic technique skillfully deployed, witty, compassionate, insightful, colloquial with a touch of erudition, occasionally provocative and even testy. Of monastic life he said:

> We must go back to some of the basic ideas, and look at them ourselves, and what I'll try to do as we go along is say, here are some of these basic ideas and show you where you can go back and meditate on them yourselves, put you in contact with sources so that you can work on them yourselves.
>
> Well, okay. Let's have a little dialogue: What's the essence of monastic vocation; what's the monastic vocation? Brother Bosco? "Seeking God." Seeking God; you see, what's the difference between saying it's silence and saying it's seeking God? Silence doesn't give you the essence, it gives you one of the means. So then, when you talk about the essence of life, you get right into the heart of it and say what it's for, and when you're talking about the means, like silence, you're talking about how you get to the end, see, how you get to what you're trying to do. So there's a question here of means and ends. The end in view is the thing that we're after; well, now, what we're going to talk about first of all is this end in view. What are we in the monastery for?
>
> Now this is something to which there is not a real simple answer; you say seeking God, certainly, but you see, that's a

good answer, fine, it's as good an answer as you can give. But then once you've given the answer you've still got to go deeper into it, you see, and actually, what you do is you spend your whole life trying to find out what it means to seek God. You don't know when you come in, and you don't even know when you're on your deathbed. After you die you find God, and then you know what the whole story was all about. You come and you seek God all your life and then you die: see, that's the monastic life, the monastic life as a whole. The monastic life isn't something you live for a week. The monastic life you live until you die.

Paradoxically, Merton's increased contact with people encouraged an even stronger need for solitude. He longed for the life of a hermit and the solitude and silence it would afford. He would attempt to convince his superiors of the wisdom of his longing. Nicholls reflects:

He began eventually to see a possible solution within the framework of the Cistercian life. Perhaps he could live as a hermit while still belonging to the community of Gethsemani and the Cistercian order. The Benedictine Rule provided for such a possibility, but it had not been invoked in modern times. Merton sought permission from his abbot to set up a hermitage for himself in the grounds of the abbey and live there. Permission was at first refused and then extended by stages.

From 1965 until his departure for Asia in 1968, Merton was living as a hermit in the small concrete block house in the grounds of the abbey originally constructed by Merton and his novices on the pretext of having somewhere to meet with ecumenical guests. Merton's was the first officially sanctioned experiment in the solitary life within the Cistercian order in modern times. Merton was no ordinary contemplative. He sought a creative marriage of the active and the passive, the transcendent and temporal, the imaginative and the mystical.

Contemplation for Merton did not mean withdrawal in the sense of rejection; it really meant encounter with the issues of the day from the vantage point of spiritual balance.

Merton wrote of some of the pressing social concerns of the America of the '60s: 'A letter arrived stamped with the slogan "The US Army: Key to Peace." No army is the key to peace, neither the US army nor the Soviet army nor any other. No great nation has the key to anything but war. Power has nothing to do with peace. The more men build up military power the more they violate peace and destroy it.'

Merton had discovered early on that he needed to remain as vigilant inside the monastery as he had outside against the authoritarian instincts that threaten genuine spiritual freedom. Having fought his war against the Trappist authorities and lost—it was an easy capitulation, because of the vow of obedience—he was delighted by the move on the part of his Gethsemani superiors to at least in part recognize his need for some solitary time. A small hermitage was built in the fall of 1960 for the express purpose of *rencontres* and dialogue with Protestant clergy and academics, but it was also understood that Merton could use it for private purposes on occasion as well. This concession was a small but meaningful one. But if it was intended to placate Merton or subdue his need to speak to the people of his time, it was an unsuccessful ruse. Merton would not be silenced. As he admitted to his friend Wilbur "Ping" Ferry, a contemplative monk should have "a quiet but articulate" place in the discussions of the day.

The consolations of withdrawal from the world, a premier motivation of his early monastic years, were waning fast. Merton's monastic rebellion would need to be further mutated; he would need to redefine his foundational "no" to the world. This redefinition was arrestingly telescoped around the pressing issue of peace.

As the 1960s unfolded and the Cold War heated up, Merton found it increasingly difficult to subscribe to what he once dubbed "the monastery as dynamo concept." This pious notion conceived of the monastery as a spiritual power centre, generating grace and blessings, with each monk performing his required spiritual tasks unquestioningly, and all working together in holy harmony under one head. By the early 1960s, Merton had repudiated this notion unequivocally, and had come to believe that the monk as spiritual cog in the great machine was a vicious caricature of monasticism. The idea that Merton had earlier embraced with equanimity, if not zeal—that the monk is called to sacrifice his individuality—he now rejected. He now felt that the elimination of the individual voice in the mass society of the 20th century was an evil that must be denounced—that the individual voice must be heard, and heard loudly.

All the more reason why Merton found the suppression of his own contributions in the public arena of the matter of peace a particularly onerous burden to bear. Merton refused to toe the official Catholic line; he was increasingly pacifist in his thinking, though never a pure one, arguing vigorously against the "just war" theory that originated with Saint Augustine and was then refined by Saint Thomas Aquinas, and had been standard Catholic teaching for centuries. To Merton, episcopal timidity could not be justified with nuclear incineration on the horizon.

His superiors were disturbed by Merton's increasingly forceful and decidedly political reflections on peace in the nuclear era. The Trappist authorities in both Europe and in Kentucky, under pressure from the American bishops but also out of their own sense of disquiet, ordered Merton to publish no more articles about peace issues. He obeyed, but only just. For some time he had been writing pointed, highly critical letters to various correspondents, which he had gestetnered or mimeographed, collated, compiled, and widely but circumspectly circulated with the help of obliging younger monks, like the poet Brother Paul Quenon:

> This was the time when many of his writings were banned. He was writing letters to many significant figures and I often found myself slowing down the process of mimeographing simply because I kept reading what he wrote. It was really an intense thing for me to read this profoundly prophetic and important voice in a context where everyone else seemed to be dangerously oblivious to the kinds of issues he was addressing.

They came to be known as the Cold War Letters and they are 111 in number, written between October 1961 and October 1962. The definitive order prohibiting him to write any further on politics and peace issues was enacted in April 1962. His experiment in *samizdat* or underground literature was over. At least officially.

Merton castigated the monastic authorities for reducing the monk to a supine prayer producer with no function other than to obey the "purposes and objectives of an ecclesiastical bureaucracy" and to "affirm his total support of officialdom." To Merton, for whom monasticism was always a type or form of rebellion, the figure of the monk as portrayed by his superiors did violence not only to his sense of self, but to his very understanding of monastic spirituality in both its primitive and contemporary expressions. He watched with horror the gradual and effective transformation of a community of contemplative monks into an industry: Trappist Corp.

For all his rebellious instincts and temperament, Merton possessed a generous and unassuming humility. Sister Thérèse

Lentfoehr, one of his closest confidantes, a poet friend of many years and the author of a study of his poetry, *Words and Silence*, recalls his humanity and deep warmth:

> I would say he was a very warm person, and a very simple person. I guess all the great are simple. And when he spoke to you his eyes were very special, blue-gray eyes—I think the French call it *perle*, don't they, and he would, well, you felt you were the only person in the world, I think, when he talked to you; he gave you so much attention, he would just concentrate on you, and very brotherly, very safe, familiar, and that was the way he was. Now in his letters, he was, well, a real friend and he gave me a lot of spiritual counsel, spiritual direction, and then shared his inner self with me, especially in spiritual matters.

Merton's former secretary, Silvanus, for many years a Vancouver Island potter, confirms Lentfoehr's assessment of Merton's character, but underlines his comic and witty side:

> What sort of a man was he to work for, what was he like personally, was he easy to get along with? Oh, he was very easy to get along with. When he was working seriously at his work, he didn't like interruptions of people coming in with stupid questions. He was kind of impish in his character; he liked to joke a lot. I remember one time the novices were going out to work and he passed us in the Jeep and without saying anything, signed 'Look, no hands, no hands!' and the next day in the refectory he knelt down and there was complete silence and he said, 'My fathers and brothers, I accuse myself of wrecking the Jeep.' He was a terrible driver, not very practical.
>
> On one hand we see a man who required and needed, desired, great solitude, great aloneness; on the other hand, it must have been difficult because of the constant stream of people coming, the correspondence that came, and the interruptions

he must have had in his solitude. He always spoke about the conflict between being a contemplative and a poet, between being a hermit or a writer, and I don't think he ever came to a solution on that, but there were hundreds of people coming from different parts of the world, wanting to see him, but they sort of protected him, so otherwise he would have never written the books that he did write.

There are some critics of Merton's monastic life who would dismiss it as insular, withdrawn, escapist. Religious Studies professor and author Mary Jo Weaver knew of Merton's awareness of the "terrible balance."

I think Merton exactly knew that monasticism leads to a sort of self-centeredness and he wouldn't permit himself to do that; one of the interesting things about Merton is that he can articulate the way of negation or the withdrawn kind of aspect of religious life, and then articulate the way of affirmation and involvement and activity. It's not so important, I think, that he lived both those things—all of us embody one or more paradoxes in our lives—but he could articulate both of those to an exquisite degree, and I think that makes him the paradigmatic monk of the twentieth century.

Some people say Merton is a prophet. I wouldn't; I would call Merton a critic, a good social critic, a forerunner, a pioneer, maybe, in some ways. A prophet to me is someone who really is almost violent, I guess; I'm an Elijah that way, when Elijah calls for the God who comes in fire; drama, violence, the person who's inspired to speak or to deliver God's judgment on a situation. More Flannery O'Connor than Thomas Merton.

But on war and peace Merton could be prophetic at the same time as he played the role of critic, expressing his concerns for the war-ravaged East. He spoke to his novices of the possible visit of a Buddhist monk who had come to America from Viet Nam suing for peace.

> I don't want to raise any hopes or anything like that, but we were talking about the Viet Nam Buddhists; well, one of the top leaders of the Viet Nam Buddhist monks is in this country and he's traveling around with a friend of mine and there's a chance he might be down here next weekend. So I don't know if Reverend Father will let him in, but those guys are incarnate devils, you don't want an incarnate devil in the place, do you? But anyway, if Reverend Father lets him, maybe he'll give the talk next Sunday afternoon, I don't know. But he probably won't, he'll probably be in Louisville next Sunday afternoon, might be out here on Saturday, so, let's hope . . . I can tell you his name, it's Thích Thanh Từ, or something like that. But pray for him anyway. I don't know what he's doing, he's going to tell his side.

Merton's wide ecumenicity of view, expansive tolerance, and non-ideological commitment to justice, peace and dialogue remained constants throughout the last decade of his life.

But if the world was in torment and the monastery in ferment, Merton's personal life was to go in a direction few, including himself, could have anticipated: he fell in love.

Merton deplored the public perception that the monk was a special kind of human being, somehow gratefully free of those ordinary and meddlesome features of life like sexual temptation, pettiness, ambition, acquisitiveness, and so on. Nothing could be further from the truth, but he knew that he had himself contributed to that very perception in some of his earlier writings, with their ethereal tone and pious certainties. The notion that the monk was in some way a rarefied creature, sanctified and other-worldly, distressed him acutely. In a key passage in his journal *Conjectures of a Guilty Bystander*, he records a particular moment in Louisville, an epiphany, when he rejoices not in his exceptionality, his difference from humanity, his unique ontological status, but rather in his rich commonality with others:

> In Louisville, at the corner of Fourth and Walnut, in the center of the shopping district, I was suddenly overwhelmed with the realization that I loved all those people, that they were mine and I theirs, that we could not be alien to one another even though we were total strangers. It was like waking from a dream of separateness, of spurious self-isolation in a special world, the world of renunciation and supposed holiness. The whole illusion of a separate holy existence is a dream.

Although this diary entry starkly underscores his new awareness, liberating awareness, of his ordinariness, his shared humanity, he would have another experience that would both deepen and complicate this "at-oneness" with the rest of the species.

Merton was soon to discover that the idea of the monk "living detached on a special lane" was about to be imploded. The year 1966 was to be a watershed year for Merton, the year in which he fell wildly in love with a young nurse. It was to be "a time of gruesome yet beautiful alienation," a time when the two lovers were to "spin in space like empty capsules." It would prove the single greatest challenge to his continuing identity as a monk.

Prior to his meeting the young nurse, M. (as she has been identified by biographers and editors), Merton was increasingly aware that he had yet to achieve a level of maturity in relation to his understanding of women, that his past misalliances were to be righted, that his arrested psychosexual integration was yet to be accomplished, and that he displaced the feminine side of his personality. He needed to bring something like closure to his emotionally fractured past.

By 1965 he began to speak quite candidly about his self-ishness, his inability to love, his poor self-esteem, his failure to realize that the girls he flirted and cavorted with had loved him, at least for a time. He became increasingly occupied with thinking and writing about his sexuality. His diary entries on the subject are neither coy nor elliptical, but direct and unnervingly honest in their expressions of regret, shame and longing. He revisits his past and scours the amorous landscape for opportunities missed or abused. He tries to make sense of the sexual quagmire of his past and juxtaposes the sordid with the pure in a romantic's desperate effort to recover something of innocent love.

Throughout his life, Merton needed women. Earlier, his pattern had been to behave, he would have us believe, like a roué, and later, of course, like an ascetic. Either way it was a form of flight, and it was time for him to face the consequences. The heart must have its way.

The psychosomatic illnesses that plagued him throughout most of his monastic life were the clearest bodily sign of his inner division. It was time for radical healing.

It was not that Merton avoided women. Quite the contrary. He valued long and stimulating relationships with women wherein they exercised variously the roles of confidante, sister, adviser and soulmate, but not lover. Appropriate, considering his vocational vows. But incomplete.

The list of Merton's women friends—friendships nurtured by meticulous and honest correspondence—is illustrative of his wide range of interests; the friends were Roman Catholic religious and lay women, professional scholars and writers, established and unknown. The list is impressive in its composition and variety, but it is possible to identify several women with whom he had a special attachment and who played, singly and collectively, a critical role in shaping and maturing the often female-shy monk of Gethsemani. The list includes Raissa Maritain, poet and mystic; Angela Collins, Carmelite prior; Mary Luke Tobin, former Superior-General of the Sisters of Loretto; Hildegard Goss-Mayr, peace activist; June Yungblut, civil rights activist; Etta Gullick, spiritual writer; Thérèse Lentfoehr, poet and professor; Nora Chadwick, scholar and expert on monasticism; Rosemary Radford Ruether, theologian and writer; Joan Baez, composer and folksinger; and many others. He had friends galore, but something was missing. Something had to give.

His episode of the heart began after recovery from back surgery in a Louisville hospital in March of 1966 and would continue for several months, concluding definitively by the fall of the same year following a ceremony of recommitment as a monk of Gethsemani.

It was a time of deep and swirling emotion; it was a time of confusion and confounding of the old certainties; it was a time of trial and conflict over the direction he should take next; it was a time of sexual excitation, intellectual rationalization, vexing guilt, energizing hope and existential dread.

It was a time when Merton lived in his skin, on the edge, intensely. If his sexual risks were foolish, his indiscretions unfathomable, his deceptions ignoble, in the end his love for M.—and it was love, not a mid-life crisis, an obsession, an infatuation—then it is important to contextualize this event in his life as a whole. The months they had together—fleeting, for sure, given their respective duties—unfolded at first combustively and then settled into a period of an almost desperate serenity, a sweet denial, and it was clear to them both, but especially to Merton, that it would need to come to an end.

And it did.

Merton recommitted to his vows as a monk of Gethsemani. M. and he connected only sporadically, and then not at all. Like everything he did, he wrote about being a priest with a woman—in several journals as well as in poetry—with unsparing honesty, self-critique and wonder. Yes, wonder. Merton came to understand, perhaps for the first time, that he could be loved by another and that he could love; that he could learn something of what it means to be vulnerable to another, and he would discover the reciprocity of love.

The scholar and editor of volume six—1966-1967—of the *Restricted Journals of Thomas Merton*, Christine Bochen, provides a chronology, summary and assessment of Merton's affair with M.:

> In his journals—restricted at this point and utterly confidential—Merton reflects on the early days in the hospital that March of 1966, expressing something of the intensity of their relationship, something of its wonder, something of the joy and the passion that he feels. But even in those early weeks of their relationship, especially from mid-April to May, there is increasingly interwoven with the passion, the excitement and the gratitude for this relationship a deep sense of concern, an awareness of the fact that it represents not only a tension with his commitment to solitude and the life that he has chosen as a monk, and that it represents a threat to that very life. And so, in the months of May and June we find Merton in his journals alternating between peaks and high moments and then low moments when he is deeply anguished over the implications of the relationship and his future as a monk.
>
> Soon, in June, sometimes indiscreet, perhaps imprudent contacts on the telephone are discovered. He's overheard in a conversation by one of his fellow monks, who then immediately reports the conversation to the abbot. And so one might say that Merton is forced to a reconsideration. But he is also moving to this juncture. It isn't as though I think the abbot has

introduced a theme that Merton has never considered, because he is aware of the two rude facts in his life: his commitment to his vocation and his love for M.

When the Abbot calls Merton to his office and offers his advice, Merton knows that the relationship must come to an end, and he more or less complies, fudging a bit in the process. There are some further meetings between M. and him when he has the opportunity to go to Louisville, and there are the ongoing letters and calls, but it is moving to its closing. By September he has made his resolution to remain a monk, which he expresses in a symbolic and ritualistic way by recommitting in the presence of the abbot, pledging to live a life of solitude as long as his health permits.

It is over. The episode of the heart is over. But never to be forgotten. As official biographer Michael Mott notes:

> There are certain things that are very clear. It was a very genuine love affair. It developed out of a very sentimental situation into a love affair, emphasizing the word "love." It taught Thomas Merton something that he had always been uncertain about. He writes in his journal that he had not been very good with women, probably hadn't been. And he writes that he is terrified of rejection. Men who are terrified of rejection are not usually serious lovers, because they are so afraid that they are going finally to be rejected that they don't give of themselves. Merton gave of himself. And as he was able to give of himself in that way, he never again doubted that he was lovable, that he could be loved, nor did he doubt ever again that he could in turn love.

It was soon to be time for a new adventure; it was time to finally go East. The East of Brahmachari, of Chakravarty, of Suzuki, of the various mystics and holy men he had been reading for years. In fact, one could say he was going home.

For many years, he was prevented from travelling great distances—in fact, Merton's trips outside the monastery, with the exception of one to Collegeville, Minnesota, and one to New York City, were limited to Louisville. So when he received an invitation to address a gathering of monastics in December of 1968 in Bangkok, his new abbot, Flavian Burns, readily assented.

Prior to the big Asian journey—he planned to visit Ceylon (now Sri Lanka), India, Thailand and Japan—Merton spent some time travelling in the United States, including to Chicago, San Francisco, Oregon, Alaska and New Mexico. Naturally, he kept diaries recording his impressions and thoughts during all these trips.

But it was the Asian trip that proved the most decisive, if not definitive. As his dear friend and the contributing editor of his posthumously published *Asian Journal*, Amiya Chakravarty remembers:

> He had already studied a lot of Buddhism, Hinduism and Zen. But in India, he acquainted himself more deeply with those traditions, he was proceeding further in that direction, when death cut him short. But already, he had seen the Dalai Lama, the ex-king and religious head of Tibet, and had very deep and noble conversations with him as to the meaning of silence and prayer; then he came to Calcutta, back to meet artists and intellectuals and religious leaders, and got across his own point of view of an ecumenical nature, that the time has come that the faiths of the world should know each other, not by giving up what they have, but by adding to what they can receive.
>
> Did knowing Merton have an effect on my life as a Hindu? Yes, undoubtedly. That was a tremendous event for me personally, not only a change, but a transformation of outlook: that somebody from so far away, from another culture and tradition,

should be so near in spirit to what we conceive to be having the loftiest, even the sublime. So when I saw in him a kindred spirit, from another continent, across the ocean, you can imagine what profound impact it had on me as a person.

Merton died by accidental electrocution in Bangkok, Thailand, at the age of 53, 27 years to the day after he entered the monastery. The wandering monk ended his earthly travels with a flourish, an unpredictable gesture, an unnerving surprise. He would have laughed at his death, for he had a grand passion for deflating the serious and mocking the grave. We are the poorer for his death, and the richer for his wisdom.

2

Window, Tower and Circle:
The Poetic Merton

A TRAPPIST MONK vowed to silence and later a hermit yearning for solitude, Thomas Merton spoke to the world through his writings. From the seclusion of the Kentucky hills, Merton authored more than 50 books on both religious and secular matters, hundreds of articles and reviews, and a correspondence so vast that in his later years he would need a suitcase to pick up his mail. Although Merton's writings ranged from novels to religious meditations to letters to biographies of saints, it was with his journals and poetry that he was most comfortable as a writer. His first published book was a volume of verse issued in 1944. But it was his bestselling autobiography, *The Seven Storey Mountain*, that established his reputation as a writer.

Donald Grayston comments on the import of this bracing work of youth:

The Seven Storey Mountain made an immense splash when it was first published, and with the enormous popular success came letters, which moved Merton very much by their seriousness. Soon, however, he began to react against the involvement which being a writer demanded of him. You know that bit in *The Seven Storey Mountain* where he says, "There's this double, he followed me into the monastery, he walks around behind me, his name is

Thomas Merton, and people are continually asking him to write books." And at first he wanted to strangle Thomas Merton, and just be Father Louis [his name in religious life—as was then the custom, it was a name drawn from the list of the holy ones; in his case, as befits a child of France, Saint Louis IX, the saintly French monarch] for the rest of his life. But Thomas Merton had too much life in him to be, you know, quietly strangled in the monastery. And so he came to terms with this problem between writing and contemplation, a problem that he had to deal with himself—and he came to the conclusion that writing could be a vehicle for his spirituality, and that therefore he would make the best of it.

I think it remains a very, very important book, because it demonstrates how far he advanced. It's the foundation volume of his autobiographical corpus, and without reading it, a person wouldn't realize just how far he came through *The Sign of Jonas* and *Conjectures of a Guilty Bystander* to *The Asian Journal*. The later books are light years away from the triumphalist tone of *The Seven Storey Mountain*, and yet, at the same time, it remains very human, very personal, very fallible, and so many sections are freshly written.

I guess its major fault is that it's not all of a piece. It's a chunk of undigested scholasticism and then a chunk of fairly well reflected on human experience, but they aren't really integrated. It may have been his sense of futility at having ended up even in the monastery doing what he was doing outside the monastery: becoming a writer. Combined with the self-emptying which the book's writing and publication involved, to precipitate his 16 months of depression in 1949–50. Out of this he emerged mature and whole, and after that time, as far as he was concerned, right to the end of his life, *The Seven Storey Mountain* was definitely behind him.

Two years before his death, he expressed his realization of the need to be free of its effects. It was due, he said, to a book he wrote 30 years ago—in fact, it was only 20; obviously, he was pushing it farther back—that he had himself become a sort of stereotype of the world-denying contemplative, the man who spurned New York, spat on Chicago, tromped on Louisville, heading for the woods with Thoreau in one pocket, John of the Cross in another, and holding the Bible open at the Apocalypse. This personal stereotype was probably his own fault, and something he will have to try to demolish on occasion.

The year before his death, in another crack at such a demolition, he remarked, in response to an interviewer's question, that he would use *The Seven Storey Mountain* as a point of departure and that he was glad he could depart from it and keep on moving. He had, after all, left the book behind many years ago. Certainly it was a book, he observed, and it said a great deal of what he felt he had to say at the time, but if he had to do it again it would be handled in a very different way. Unfortunately, the book was a bestseller, and became a kind of edifying legend or something—there's that word 'legend'—that is a dreadful fate. He was doing his best to live it down, but the legend was stronger than he was. Nevertheless, he argued that he maintained his basic human right not to be turned into a Catholic myth for children in parochial schools.

He was resisting the exploitation of his personal myth as an exclusively Catholic myth, feeling the need, or as he put it, the basic human right to claim his myth for himself, which included the right of revision and development. So although he could not bring his autobiographical chariot down from its permanent place in the sun, he could and did parachute back to Earth. There he took up once again the editing of the self by means of three journals: *The Sign of Jonas*, *Conjectures of a Guilty Bystander* and *The Asian Journal*. He felt that through these he had been successful, at least to his own satisfaction, in his task of re-editing.

These journals constitute the ongoing autobiography: *The Seven Storey Mountain* continued. Merton was an intensely personal writer. With little taste for the driest of abstractions, and possessed of a keen eye for the uncommon yet unacknowledged epiphanies of the divine at the very heart of the ordinary, Merton examined every thought, feeling and impression through the lens of his own experience. The monk who sought the elimination of the "I" was the very same writer who nurtured it. In sum: the paradox of the divided self, the marriage of heaven and hell.

Merton was an essayist, poet, calligrapher, photographer, controversialist, social and political commentator, editor, anthologist, translator and sometime cartoonist. He was a religious thinker, not a theologian per se, a religious visionary in the manner of William Blake, a correspondent of gargantuan energies, and a belle-lettrist of startling virtuosity. But we continue to read him, primarily, for the same reason that we read Saint Augustine, Blaise Pascal and Simone Weil: the personal voice, the personal revelation, the disclosing or confessional tone.

It is not surprising, then, that Thomas Merton's more explicitly autobiographical writings continue to enjoy the greater popularity in his formidable canon. Although Merton did try his hand with other genres, like the hagiographies of Mother M. Berchmans and Saint Lutgarde of Aywieres—published, respectively, as *Exile Ends in Glory* and *What Are these Wounds?*—and although he did write a systematic exposition of the ascetical theology of Saint John of the Cross known as *The Ascent to Truth*, Merton's preference was clearly for the self-exploratory possibilities of both pure and disguised autobiography.

Merton's arduous quest for the real self, the true self, could be seriously undertaken only once he resolved to vigorously examine the myriad masks, the numberless faces he donned in both the public and the private realm. And so we have the tantalizing striptease of the would-be anonymous monk: Merton's strategy of disclosure, for all its presumed candour and spontaneity, is a deftly handled process involving stringent editing and careful construction. Merton strips with modesty.

Autobiography is a mode of theological investigation; it is also Merton's *via negativa,* a way of sundering and reconstituting, a way of purgation and integration. The voluble eremite draped with the mantle of enclosure redefines silence through the power of words. He lives, as he would have it, in the "belly of a paradox," and he invites the reader to travel with him on his *peregrinatio,* his going "forth into strange places," in order to better understand the mystery of the "I." He will explore the dread region of the Shadow—both exterior and interior—and the cadaver minutely dissected for public show will be none other than himself.

Merton's autobiographical writings may smack of rank exhibitionism, and undoubtedly the lonely child of Montauban, Cambridge and Columbia can be divined at the very heart of many an emotional and spiritual maelstrom, but there is, more importantly, a luminous, grace-suffused honesty about Merton's self-disclosures that continue to engage the interest of mature and critical readers.

Merton's honesty compelled him to chronicle his search for the true self in such a way that his readers could and can continue to vicariously share in both the light and dark sides of spiritual growth.

One of the more obvious reasons for Merton's almost manic determination to continue his autobiography was simply his discomfort with the legacy of *The Seven Storey Mountain.* The rewriting, the reinvention, of the monk-poet of Gethsemani became, after the 1948 publication of *Mountain*, a spiritual, intellectual and moral necessity. Merton was no longer simply the "*Seven Storey Mountain* man"; he was evolving into a "guilty bystander," the silent sentinel on the borders of the Apocalypse, the incarnational poet assisting at the reparation of the damaged word. Merton the diarist helps us to see the radical remaking of one of the "burnt men."

As a diarist, Merton recorded a fully catholic range of subjects. He wrote of the various hues and contours of the clouds, of the flora and fauna to be found on the vast acreage of the Gethsemani estate, of the litany of characters to be found within and adjacent to the monastic enclosure, of the variety of sounds to be heard in the Gethsemani woods, and of the changing of the seasons in the Kentucky hillside.

Merton's enthusiasm for a new book, a just discovered author, a fascinating idea, would jostle with cynical asides and sardonic humour on the same page. His diary entries were a means of self-exploration, a mode of earnest dialogue with the anonymous reader and with himself. Some entries are nature cameos, some are compilations of things done or books to be read, some are introspective exercises, some mature meditations, and some are simply vehicles of frustration and anger. There are diary entries that serve as short essays, like the piece on Adolf Eichmann and Hannah Arendt's notion of the "banality of evil," and there are diary entries that function as short mystical expositions, like the piece on the *point vierge*, or virgin point.

Merton's diaries reveal the person. They are direct, sometimes intimate, and always honest, even if polished and fine-tuned for reader consumption. In this regard, the published journals—that is, those published during his lifetime and over which he had editorial control—are different from the often more lengthy, seldom discreet, often raw data that define the unpolished restricted journals. It is important that the reader keep in mind that the poet of Gethsemani was engaged in the endless task of making and remaking himself, and to that end, his published journals or diaries were subject to careful editing and rewriting. In short, the fresh voice of the diarist is a fine example of disciplined spontaneity. Merton wrote to be published.

The masks of the Gethsemani diarist are many: the monk as rebel, the monk as visionary, the monk as artist, the monk as religious thinker and public intellectual, the monk as the divided self, the monk as conscience of the nation, the monk as troublesome charge, the monk as renegade, the monk as obedient son, and the monk as guru. As an assemblage of masks, of personae, they tell us something about the essential Merton. They tell us what he would have us know during his lifetime; following his death, the publication of his restricted journals would tell us the rest.

Although all autobiography is a form of exhibitionism, it is controlled exhibitionism. Merton's diaries are not passive things: he *thinks, wills* and *feels* in his journals. They are fragments of an ongoing conversation, a vital dialogue between diarist and reader, a kind or type of spiritual direction. Their immense popularity is in part attributable to the fact that, in spite of his extraordinary gifts, he is portrayed as a common wayfarer, and his search for the true self, "to be alone with the Alone," is a search available to everyone.

Accessible to the many rather than the elite, more inclined on occasion to use slang rather than the affected discourse of the intellectual dilettante or the rarefied prose of the academic, Merton could commune with the erudite one moment and ask some visitors to bring a six-pack of Budweiser the next. Readers like the Merton of the diaries because he is without cant, exalted self-regard or magisterial pretensions.

The diary structure gave Merton the freedom he needed to roam, to finely hone the individual *pensée*, to merely alight on a subject in order to be quickly nourished and then move on to something else, to capture in aphoristic style the insights of a dense, systematic study. Although there is occasionally a dilettantish air about some of the diary entries, there is also a searching and vigorous intelligence at work. His diaries communicate his passionate struggle with the many contradictions that defined his life: the writer who is vowed to silence; the Columbia University graduate who maintains something of the bohemian spirit of his youth coupled with his status as a consecrated religious; the solitary man compelled to address the public order; the "hidden one" marked by fame.

The diaries reveal the many voices of Thomas Merton—the voice of the garden with its discipline and the voice of the field with its wildness—and, as the critic and biographer George Woodcock has observed apropos a discussion of Merton's poetry, the voice of the choir and the voice of the desert. Merton's diaries are at once seductive, disturbing, amusing and oracular. They care not a whit for consistency or for the straitjacket of logic. They are eclectic and alogical, with a heavy dose of Swiftian wit and Zen wisdom. They more often unsettle than soothe. Their homiletic power is to be found less in the grand rhetorical flourish, a stylistic tendency that Merton on occasion indulged, and more in their capacity to jar us out of the moral, intellectual and spiritual complacency of William Blake's "Single Vision."

But in the end, the diaries remind us that the spiritual enterprise in which Merton was engaged was nothing less than the supreme enterprise of emptying himself. And so, as he notes in the diary *The Vow of Conversation*, "I am aware of the need for constant self-revision and growth," and in so doing he recognized that his job and that of the church is 'to awaken in myself and in others the sense of real possibility of truth, of obedience to Him who is holy, a refusal of pretenses and servitudes, without arrogance and pride and without any specious idealism.'"

Donald Grayston weighs the worth of the Merton diaries:

Well, in terms of literary merit, I wish I knew more about diaries than I do, but they are absolutely fascinating. For instance, there's no detail too small to get into *The Sign of Jonas*, whether it's an old monk making baskets, or his indigestion, or how he reacted to a particular verse of a psalm, or, you know, a bird sitting on a branch outside his window, but in terms of development, it seems to me that there's a very marked human development—no real theological development. Literary development, well, it's much more of a piece, I mean, it has much more integrity than *The Seven Storey Mountain*; it isn't filled with ten or fifteen pages at a stretch of undigested theology, but the focus is still very much a monastic one. The focus in *The Seven Storey Mountain* of course is monastic, and the viewpoint in *The Sign of Jonas* is also very, very monastic.

[As for] *Conjectures of a Guilty Bystander*, he has integrated his monasticism by this point, and he just is a monk, that's all, and he's not worried about it, he's not worrying about leaving or going to some other monastery. One of the concerns of *The Sign of Jonas* was 'is this a good enough place for me to be a monk, or will my journey to heaven be impeded by the sound of the cheese-making machines?' because Gethsemani by that time had become such a factory, both in the sense that it was a cheese factory—they made all this Trappist cheese—and also in the human sense, that it was, it had ... there were 270 monks in a building that had been designed for I believe something around a hundred, so they were just crammed in, and Merton felt that the degree of solitude that was necessary for contemplation wasn't going to be available to him very much longer.

Well, they made a few foundations, and that took the pressure off—some of the monks went off to Utah and Georgia and other places—but in the period of *The Sign of Jonas*, up to the early '50s, he was wondering if he should be a Carthusian, and he later decided that that was a temptation and a distraction, and he put it out of his mind. And when that was out of his mind, really in a sense the whole monastic thing had been integrated. He just was a monk, and he was able to bring the monastic viewpoint to bear on various subjects. But really, his concern had moved from the monastery to the world, and the world, with all its problems and sorrows, the world which he thought he had left behind in *The Seven Storey Mountain*, that was now the focus of his interest and his concern and his compassion.

In his journals, the reader can easily happen upon an idea, an impression, a theory rich in multiple meanings, and learn that not only do the diaries reflect Merton's interest in the little thing, but often reveal a profound mind at work on the larger thing; not only a seeming inconsequential sound of nature, but an idea central to mystical vision. For example, the *point vierge*, or virgin point, which is really a metaphor for the ultimate mystical experience. It has a kind of spatial reference, and it has a temporal reference, and it has an experiential reference: you can experience the *point vierge* in terms of time—he liked to talk about the moment of pre-dawn when a couple of the birds who have seen the sun before he has begin to sing and then the sun rises. But the kind of *virgin point* of the day, and then all through *Seeds* and *New Seeds of Contemplation*, he talked about the *Centre of the Soul* or the *apex mentis*—those are some of the traditional mystic terms.

I think he took the *Centre of the Soul* because it was from Saint John of the Cross, but also it's a term that's fairly accessible to ordinary people, and he talked about passing through that Centre into God and then passing back from God through the Centre of the Soul—and he used all kinds of prepositions, he talked about abiding in the Centre, going through the Centre, moving to the Centre, going past the Centre, and so on, and that's the experiential thing. At *le point vierge*, you just are with God—and to pick up another strand of his thought—you're past images, you've just gone beyond all images and doctrines and definitions—you're just in God and with God. You come back from having gone through the *virgin point* and you are a different kind of person and in your ordinary day-to-day life you create, you write, you think, you produce calligraphies, you do various things as the kind of person who, having been through the virgin point, is a very different person from the person who has not experienced that kind of personal centering and integration.

Merton, however, remained primarily the poet, not the diarist, even when he despaired of his poetic talent or fought relentlessly with the demands on his time; he always succumbed to its allure simply because in spite of all his prayer and anxiety, he was and would remain a poet. He was a special type of poet with many masks and many voices. But at heart he was a visionary, and his poems may be divided between those of experience and those of innocence. The poems of innocence are generally lyrical, and they consist of songs, aubades, elegies or psalms. They are celebratory, reflective and evocative. Perhaps no more moving an example of this type of poem, with its clarity of feeling and power of reflection, can be found than in his elegy *For My Brother: Reported Missing in Action, 1943.*

Sweet brother, if I do not sleep
My eyes are flowers for your tomb;
And if I cannot eat my bread,
My fasts shall live like willows where you died.
If in the heat I find no water for my thirst,
My thirst shall turn to springs for you, poor traveller.

Where, in what desolate and smoky country,
Lies your poor body, lost and dead?
And in what landscape of disaster
Has your unhappy spirit lost its road?

Come, in my labor find a resting place
And in my sorrows lay your head,
Or rather take my life and blood
And buy yourself a better bed—
Or take my breath and take my death
And buy yourself a better rest.

When all the men of war are shot
And flags have fallen into dust,
Your cross and mine shall tell men still
Christ died on each, for both of us.

For in the wreckage of your April Christ lies slain,
And Christ weeps in the ruins of my spring;
The money of Whose tears shall fall
Into your weak and friendless hand,
And buy you back to your own land:

The silence of Whose tears shall fall
Like bells upon your alien tomb.
Hear them and come: they call you home.

Unlike the lyricism to be found in his poems of innocence, his poems of experience are frequently dissonant and consist of satires, anti-poems and prose poems. When he left the life of an academic in the making, a budding writer, to become a monk, he brought with him into the monastery a fear of the world that gnawed at him for some time, and he loathed his former life. His poems reflect his discontent with a society whose one ambition is the making of money and whose ultimate end is a common conflagration; a society indifferent to the innocence of the child; a society of crucifiers.

The general collapse of confidence in the inherently humane traditions of the culture that shaped the West, which emerged as a consequence of the devastation of the Second World War, contributed no small part in confirming Merton in his conviction of the world's corruption. As the thinker mellowed, the poet matured. No longer simply satisfied to judge the world and find it wanting, Merton preferred, by the late 1950s, to engage the world. He did this by offering a critique of its myths—those myths that enslave and those that liberate. Such a tactic was to become his major preoccupation as Merton worked out his strategy of vision—his plan of restoration. Merton discovered that there is no better way as a poet to assist at this restoration or recovery of paradise than through a rectification of vision or a right ordering of our seeing. Merton was convinced that the premier reason for our spiritual and intellectual disarray can be found in our collective inability to actually see creation, to actually see the truth. Victims of a mindless abstractionism, humans flail above the world of reality with the big stick of reason, battering the concrete and the individual into submission. In the age of the mass person, it is imperative that the voice of the final arbiter of freedom, the poet, be heard with clarity:

Where is the marvelous thief
Who stole whole harvests from the angry sun
And sacked, with his bright sight, the land?

Where he lies dead, the quiet earth unpacks him
And wind is waving in the earth's revenge:
Fields of barley, oats and rye.

Where is the millionaire
Who squandered the bright spring?
Whose lies played in the summer evening sky
Like cheap guitars?
Who spent the golden fortunes of the fall
And died as bare as a tree?

His heart lies open as a treasury,
Filled up with grass and generous flowers.

Where is the crazy gambler
Amid the nickels of whose blood have fallen
Heavy half dollars of his last of life?
Where is he gone?

The burning bees come walk, as bright as jewels
Upon that flowering, dark sun:
The bullet wound in his unmoving lung.

Oh you who hate the gambler or his enemy,
Remember how the bees
Pay visits to the patient dead
And borrow honey from their charitable blood.

You who have judged the gambler or his enemy
Remember this, before the proud world's funeral.

    "Dirge for the Proud World"

Merton was a child, a lover and a mystic. He was also a pilgrim on a journey towards Paradise, in search of the sacred Tree of Life, going forth into the strange countries like the ancient Irish monks in his quest to be free. This journey consists of three stages. In the first, called the Stage of Initiation, Merton seeks to purify himself of his attachment to sense, in order that he may more thoroughly dedicate himself to the priorities of the soul. The author of *The Seven Storey Mountain* has little patience for the world, a world glutted by an excess of material desire, ravaged by an insatiable hate of the spiritual and fanatically determined to undermine all possibility for survival. This is the world he rejected.

In his last year in the world, 1941, Merton saw the coming peril and knew that the cry that terrifies the sentinel was at hand. Judgment was near; and if not the general judgment, then at least a private apocalypse. And so the pilgrim yearns for Jerusalem. And he finds it even if only temporarily in the hills and valleys of Kentucky. The calamities of the world, the wounds of the cities and the ruins of once proud lives are rendered quiet, healed and won by those who have wandered like the moaning trains and live now in the house of God. The monks of Gethsemani—who, Merton writes in a poem called "A Letter to My Friends," loved the holy desert, "Where separate strangers, hid in their disguises / Have come to meet, by night, the quiet Christ"—cannot but be conscious of the irony of their vocation to heal and make whole when once the name Gethsemani, the garden of pain, evoked wretched betrayal at worst and weakness at best. But now Merton writes in the same poem,

> And look, the ruins have become Jerusalems,
> And the sick cities re-arise, like shining Sions!
> Jerusalems, these walls and rooves,
> These bowers and fragrant sheds,
> Our desert's wooden door,
> The arches, and the windows, and the tower!

Windows are a recurring symbol in this period of Merton's journey. In his poem "The Storm at Night," the windows—the senses, the Blakean doors of perception—are flailed by temptation and the hail of discord. He writes,

> All night the wind sings likes a surf
> Filling our windows with the flailing hailstorm.
> The fearful prisoner lies bound
> In blankets and bodily sleep . . .

But the senses can be transformed; they can be rendered at peace with the soul, as transparent panes of beauty and harmony. He writes in his poem "Clairvaux,"

> Pouring in sun through rib and leaf and flower of foliate window
> Gardening the ground with shadow-light, with day and night
> In every lovely interplay.

The senses are prepared in the Garden of Clairvaux to be enriched by the soul, to be ultimately subsumed by the soul so that praise may be offered the One in unity rare and inestimable. But this can be achieved only when the enticements of the world, the allurements of the flesh, the deflections of inattention and thoughtlessness from the monk's holy resolve, which intrude upon the domain of a soul recollected in solitude, are finally laid to rest. Deeply conscious of the spiritual misrule of the lords of enterprise, corporation and syndicate, and the grave disquiet of the harried masses,

Merton longed for the first fruits in their quietude in the perfect arbours of stability and rule. As Clairvaux had once offered this commodious environment to a needy Europe and a fledging Cistercian Order, Gethsemani now offers to an impoverished America: "Hidden in this heaven-harbour/ Wood-cradle valley, narrow and away from men" a sanctuary in a turbulent society, a "model of all solitudes", where distraction, appetite, and self-aggrandizement have no hearing, a "picture of contemplation and of love, the figure of all prayer/Clairvaux cloister."

Gethsemani is paradise. But not quite. Although the integration of the senses is fused into one sustained paean and, unhindered by the encroachments of time and crass necessity, is assured by the resolved contemplative soaked in grace, the monk poet has just emerged from the first stage. The senses no longer order the life of the Christian; they are now the windows of the soul. The senses are no longer the windows of the night train, reflecting the unreason of a rainy midnight; they are now the foliate windows of a cloistered Clairvaux.

English literature scholar Ernest Griffin underscores the centrality of the symbol of the window in Merton's early poetry:

> If I may summarize Merton's use of the window, we have, I think, three main elements: the window as an eye, through which the divine looks upon man's life; the window which reveals a universal formal or ritual pattern; and the window whose powerful brilliance shines through it, steals away our secrecy and uplifts us. Merton's first use of window in his poetry, beyond a casual reference, is in an early poem entitled *The Blessed Virgin Mary Compared to a Window*. This poem is not so much a comparison of conceit as an absorption in which Mary becomes a window for God.

Because my will is simple as a window
And knows no pride of original earth,
It is my life to die, like glass, by light:
Slain in the strong rays of the bridegroom sun.

Because my love is simple as a window
And knows no shame of original dust,
I longed all night, (when I was visible) for dawn my death:
When I would marry day, my Holy Spirit:
And die by transsubstantiation into light.

For light, my lover, steals my life in secret.
I vanish into day, and leave no shadow
But the geometry of my cross,
Whose frame and structure are the strength
By which I die, but only to the earth,
And am uplifted to the sky my life. . . .

Because I die by brightness and the Holy Spirit,
The sun rejoices in your jail, my kneeling Christian . . .

Merton uses this triadic pattern in various ways, so that what
begins as a scene as simple and true as innocence becomes
profound and complex, and sometimes corrupted. The chapel
window may, in the permission of a literary context, become
an internal soul window, whereby the looked upon is invited to
join, as it were, with the one who looks in on him. Or the window
may become blinded, as he says, by a false light or a reflection.
Here, in an ironic version, are the three elements in a poem,
which is not a poem of praise, but rather of prophecy, and the
scene is not a chapel, but the state of modern urban life. It is
also a fairly early poem, published in *A Man in the Divided Sea*
(1946). It is an aubade, a form that Merton used a number of
times. This one is entitled "Aubade—The City." Conventionally,
an aubade is a cheery poem, maybe about a rosy dawn and the

promise of a beautiful new day. Now we happen to know what Merton thinks of the modern city; the title in itself indicates at least a touch of irony.

> Now that the clouds have come like cattle
> To the cold waters of the city's river,
> All the windows turn their scandalized expression
> Toward the tide's tin dazzle,
>
> And question, with their weak-eyed stare,
> The riotous sun.

In the middle of the poem, we have the windows involved in the design image, denoting not peace, but disunity:

> All down the faces of the buildings
> Windows begin to close
> Like figures in a long division

And finally we have the light delving into the secrecy of our being, but now the illumination or the destruction of our secrecy is feared. With this poem, in relation to the poems of praise, we have another theme develop through the window imagery, and that is, crudely put, the chapel window versus the city window, and this becomes the counterpoint in several later poems.

In the second stage, called the Stage of Translucence, Merton seeks enlightenment or illumination, concentrating exclusively on the work of spiritual intuition. The symbol that best represents his struggle at this stage is the tower. The significance of the tower is equivocal. In his early poems, Merton often alludes to the tower as a stronghold of faith, a guarantor of solitude, a symbol of creative isolation, and a summoner of the distant and the dead. In his poem "St. Malachy," Merton writes, "Two bells in the steeple /

Talk faintly to the old stranger / And the tower considers his waters."

Called to share on his feast day with those who play to him the plainsong of the giant Gregory, Malachy must leave the silence of his history to partake of the silence of the monks' witness. The abbey has more than the church tower, however; it has, well situated on a not easily accessible knob but a few miles from the monastery, a fire tower abandoned by the rangers. Here, for a few short hours, was Merton's much longed for hermitage. From it he could survey, and I quote from his poem "In the Rain and the Sun,"

> Four or five mountains come walking
> To see the little monks' graves.
> Flying the neutral stones I dwell between cedars
> And see the countries sleeping in their beds;
> Lands of the watermen, where poplars bend.

Securely preserved from the clamour and clangour of a spiritually disabled society in the citadel of Gethsemani, and granted a privileged solitude on occasion in a secluded tower, Merton intuited a fundamental disorder, a consequence of the fall, whereby the servant of truth—the Word—had been uprooted from the ground of transcendence. This disorder and its effects he understood as the curse of the tower, the Tower of Babylon. This became the central myth of his poetic vision, as Merton saw the legacy of the tower in the disharmony of peoples; the rhetoric of war and hate; the jargon of big business and legal transaction; the polemics of rapid ideologues, be they of the left or the right; the thunderous verbiage of demagogues, the skilled periphrasis of accomplished academics and the unskilled periphrasis of aspiring politicians; the crafty subterfuge of seasoned diplomats; and the Machiavellian machinations of alarmist churchmen. Rather than serving as a vehicle of truth, the Word has become a weapon of power and division; the *logos* has been betrayed ever again.

In his morality play *The Tower of Babel*, published in 1957, Merton has his leader say to the assembled workers,

> Already I see that the skies are as full of words as they are of stars. Each word becomes an instrument of war. Words are the clocks and the devils. Words are the wheels and the machines. Steel words stronger than flesh or spirit. Secret words which divide the essences of things. Last of all, the one word that strikes at the heart of creation, and dissolves it into its original nothingness. Give me possession of this one word and I will forget every other.

And the chorus screams in unison,

> "FEAR! FEAR!"

This statement is a perfect example of the psychology of fear and of power with which our century has a tragic and intimate familiarity. It is the voice of Der Fuhrer; El Caudillo; Il Duce; the petty czars of modern Russia; the imperial regents of Republican America; the vestigial potentates that was once the Ottoman Empire; the mock heroic despots of Uganda, Paraguay and Haiti; and it is the voice of intransigent union bosses. For this reason, silence is anathema and must be judged dangerous to the state.

Faced with the awesome reality of the universal abuse of language, the Christian poet must explore the possibilities of silence; the poet must find anew the roots of language, the pristine meaning of words, and in so doing, dismantle permanently the tower of sin. For Merton, the ultimate reparation of Babylon is Pentecost, and until the healing is effected, the Christian's responsibility, especially the monk-poet's, is to purify language and wait in silence for the coming whole-ness. This wholeness shall be realized in a perfect city, built on eternal foundations, and it shall stand forever, because it is built by the thought, and the silence, and the wisdom, and the power of God. And so the disarray of language shall be ended.

For Merton, the clarity of his intuition, the translucence of his understanding, signals a further integration, a deeper maturity of mind and spirit. The symbol of the tower, which earlier smacked of a youthful triumphalism, has emerged by the end of the 1950s as a personal symbol of self-forgetfulness and immersion in the Divine will.

The symbol of the tower, however, shall be sharpened and honed to a cone placed in the midst of a circle. Then shall the mystic embrace the centre, the one. And as Saint Thomas Aquinas says, "the mystic will be with him, as the alone with the alone." The symbol of the circle can be found in the final stage, called the Final Integration. It is the symbol of the unitive way of the fullness of mystical union. The dance is the most primitive of circles, the most basic of rituals. It is a celebration of the mystery of life, of the rhythm of nature, and it is a sacred primordial rite, in which the perimeters of being are defined within the boundaries of the unknown. As the Elizabethans and ancients would have it, it is the very epitome of the cosmic dance. In "Seven Archaic Images," Merton reconstructs a troglodytic *danse macabre* in which a procession to the caves, a magic door, a cauldron, a knight counsel, a winter morning, feathered images of kings and heroes, and music is fused into a wild dance of death, a circle of war, a ring of violence. This is the contemporary scene, the constant in temple history, the very mark of Cain. Opposed to it is the Dance of Life, the quiet beckoning and gentle allure of the circle of joy, the ring of solitude.

But our hearts are deadened to the sounds of silence; they are steeled to resist the warmth of contemplation. Ours is a dance of frenzy, with five-star generals singing. From Merton's 1967 epic *Cables to the Ace*:

> To sing their loud
> Steel tunes
> Those burning blues
> For body and soul
>
> "Cable 45"

it is the dance of a holocaust, "The fairy bombers/ The fatal recorders/ The electric lyres," a dance whereby all shall be consumed by fire in one apocalyptic moment.

From the posthumously published and incomplete Blakean epic *The Geography of Lograire*:

> "Now is the Creature damm'd and ramm'd into its only Center
> Into the bowels of still Eternity; its Mother's womb
> There to dwell forever unknown
> This and this only is the 'damnation'
> So much terrifying the creature
> In its dark apprehensions..."
>
> North 4: C III, "The Ranters and their Pleads"
> (London)

This is not the language of the dark night of the senses, but rather the language of demented zeal, the language of nuclear rhetoric, the language of crippling fear, the language of pointless annihilation. At the heart of the still point is perfect meaning and perfect rest and not fear in the bowels of eternity. The circle of harmony in flux, the uroboros, the circle of pure form and intellectual symmetry is akin to the dance of life—ordered, creative and free.

In the final stage of Merton's mystical journey, the journey toward ultimate freedom, the circle becomes the mandala, the symbol of perfect integration and spiritual harmony. He had occasional premonitions that he would die soon, and this perhaps unsettling intuition found expression in his work, sometimes consciously and at other times unconsciously. In *Cables to the Ace*, published a year before his death, Merton envisions the call of the East, the Asia of his death, in the image of a mandala:

> Better to study the germinating waters of my wood
> And know this fever; or die in a distant country
> Having become a pure cone
> Or turn to my Eastern abstinence
> With that old, inscrutable love cry
> And describe a perfect circle.

> "Cable 74"

That the East represented the fulfillment of a dream, a yearning for knowledge, and growth for Merton can be readily attested to by his passionate absorption of the wisdom of Eastern spirituality and his total immersion in the contemplative quest for God. His friend and confidante Sister Thérèse Lentfoehr comments on Merton's Zen mystical poetry:

> Merton, in his readings in Zen Buddhism in the mid '50s and early '60s, came upon what was to him a metaphysical parallel to this inner experience, which he found so difficult to write of. Now this he had already glimpsed in the Rhenish mystic Meister Eckhart, and it was the Japanese Zen Master Suzuki who had used Eckhart as the example of a Christian mystic. At Suzuki's request, Merton was given permission to visit him in New York in June of 1964. That was kept very quiet; he went incognito and spent two days with Suzuki. He was forbidden to call up any

of his friends and was made to stay right there on campus. But this is what he said: "It was profoundly important to me to see and experience the fact that there really is a deep understanding between myself and this extraordinary and simple man, whose books I have been reading now for about ten years with great attention."

In Eckhart, Merton had found attempts to delineate the experience of this inner awareness of God and saw parallels between the metaphysical intuition of Zen—its fullness, limitlessness and utter freedom—and the experience of the mystic. In his 1957 volume of verse, *The Strange Islands*, we have what might be called the pure metaphysical lyric—not in the manner of the 17th-century school of English poets, the so-called Metaphysicals—but in a strict philosophical sense, for Merton was dealing with 'being,' formal *esse*, the 'is-ness' of things; each thing being simply what it *is* and its unique individuality.

This delving into ontological sources makes for a certain obscurity—that was one of the criticisms of the book—but then Merton was dealing with an entity that can be experienced by intuition only, and communicated, if at all, through image and symbol. For instance, in his poem "Stranger," from *The Strange Islands*, Merton speaks of the trees, sun, rain, the last star, all simply being what they are. Merton is pre-eminently himself as poet and mystic, as he tries to capture, in image and symbol, the ineffable experience of God:

> Where no one feels
> The first drop of rain
> Or sees the last star
>
> Or hails the first morning
> Of a giant world
> Where peace begins
> And rages end:

One bird sits still
Watching the work of God:
One turning leaf,
Two falling blossoms,
Ten circles upon the pond.

One cloud upon the hillside,
Two shadows in the valley
And the light strikes home.
Now dawn commands the capture
Of the tallest fortune,
The surrender
Of no less marvelous prize!

Closer and clearer
Than any wordy master,
Thou inward Stranger
Whom I have never seen,

Deeper and cleaner
Than the clamorous ocean,
Seize up my silence
Hold me in Thy Hand!

Now act is waste
And suffering undone
Laws become prodigals
Limits are torn down
For envy has no property
And passion is none.

Look, the vast Light stands still
Our cleanest Light is One!

In a life rich with paradox, the Trappist monk vowed to stability became a wanderer, and the logic of Zen, not of the medieval schoolmen, spoke eloquently to his needs. One must travel to go nowhere. The pilgrim found his shrine in Bangkok, not in Lourdes; and in the language of interior reason, not conceptual logic. In order to more fully drink from the springs of Christian mysticism, Merton replenished himself with the waters of Thailand's soul. He did not abandon the theological and spiritual tradition of which he was so distinguished a spokesperson. The circle—the symbol of his personal fulfillment, of the consummation of his journey, the sign of his integration made perfect in the heart of Asia—was with him at the very beginning, not yet mature, not yet perfected, but the sign of what was to be. As early as 1946, in his poem "Ode to the Present Century," he succinctly phrased his cradle of the mystical life in but a few lines:

> Turn all your hunger to humility and to forgiveness,
> Forsake your deserts of centrifugal desire:
> Then ride in peaceful circles to the depths of life
> And hide you from your burning noon-day devil
> Where clean rock-water dropwise spends, and dies in rings.

He was not to deviate from this cradle in any radical sense for the course of his monastic life. The window, the tower and the circle; the symbols of his journey towards integration do not supplant or invalidate each other. They interpenetrate, as do the Plotinian and Dionysian mystical stages. In the latter days of his life, Merton could still write with unnerving prescience, given the particulars of his electrifying death, in *Cables to the Ace* that he is "About to make my home in the bell's summit, set my mind a thousand feet high" ("Cable 87").

Throughout his life, both pre-conversion and post-conversion, Merton craved contact with a reality, transcendent and permanent; a reality that explained the poetic beauty of southern France, the sublimity of a Gerard Manley Hopkins poem, the perspicuity of a Thomistic insight, the subtlety of a Zen state. He read Aldous Huxley and William Blake in search of it. He journeyed to the heart of rustic America to discover it in the life of a monastic order. And he travelled to the Far East to learn of it from the Rinpoche, the Shaman, the Lama. "If you seek it, you do not find it." When he understood this—and the East instructed him—then and only then did the words of the Rhine mystic Eckhart strike Merton as irrefutably true. "The true word of eternity is spoken only in the spirit of the man who is himself a wilderness," or a void, or a perfect circle. In his fight against the polluters of language and of silence, the desecrators of true reason and the violators of true affection, Merton was as much the crusader as he was the poet; the prophet as the visionary. He was born a poet, he lived a poet, and he died one—alone and dreaming of wholeness—that wholeness which is known as wisdom.

3

Solitary Critic

BY TEMPERAMENT A solitary and by vocation a Trappist monk, Merton preferred the freedom of the Kentucky hills to the confinement of an American metropolis; the order and quiet of the monastery to the chaos and noise of the world. Though initially he found in the monastic enclosure an escape from the world he had come to loathe, he never formally rejected that world. As a 16-year-old schoolboy in England, he had already argued India's cause for independence. As an adolescent and young man, he developed the keen awareness of the social critic and often expressed disgust and ridicule for the institutions of the world. In the late 1930s, Merton flirted with the Communist Party, and while he later rejected Communism, many of the ideas and hopes of Karl Marx remained with him throughout his life. For Merton, joining the Abbey of Our Lady of Gethsemani was one way in which he could realize his lifelong commitment to protest, but he would realize it, he thought, through contemplation and solitude, rather than through action. While many would see an inherent contradiction in this attitude, Merton did not.

Religious Studies scholar and feminist Mary Jo Weaver comments on the seeming contradiction between the contemplative life and the life of the prophet:

I think Merton was always interested in the world and in being active in the world. As a young man he was interested in Dorothy Day and what that would be. He wanted to be a Franciscan, in poverty and in the world, and that sort of thing. And when he went to the monastery, I think what he had to do was to prepare himself somehow to take up a role in that world, in a way. And what prepared him, oddly, paradoxically, was contemplative life. He wasn't prepared by going to diplomatic school, you know, or to the Peace Corps or something like that. He was prepared by contemplative life. And the reason that that prepared him is because contemplative life helps you to see rightly, to perceive things in a certain kind of way. And out of that sort of contemplative way the peace, the *quies* as it is called, followed by mystical vision. Once you get in tune with God to that extent, you know, that kind of oneness, if you will, you're led by the logic of love, Love with a capital L, back then to seeing the world as God's handiwork, as God's creation, and being able to be active in it in a *different* kind of way.

Merton followed the course of silent action for 16 or 17 years, yet by the late 1950s he began to feel a certain uneasiness and even guilt about his silence and the atmosphere of otherworldliness prevalent in the monastery. In his diary *Conjectures of a Guilty Bystander*, Merton made explicit his involvement in the world, and reminded the reader, and perhaps more importantly the Church at large, that even bystanders are implicated in the world's doings.

Merton knew that he was a contemporary of Auschwitz, Hiroshima, Vietnam and the Watts riots, and although he was not consulted about them, he was deeply and personally implicated.

The vague feeling that by his silence he was guilty of a kind of sin had gnawed at Merton for some time, but the actual realization came to him rather suddenly in 1957. As referred to earlier, it was a pivotal experience that shattered irreversibly his sense of spiritual entitlement, his cultivated sense of exclusive destiny, his identity as exceptional witness, ontologically unlike others, withdrawn from the contaminating world of iniquity and failure. He was like others, and in that knowledge was a new and energizing liberation:

> In Louisville, at the corner of Fourth and Walnut, in the centre of the shopping district, I was suddenly overwhelmed with the realization that I loved all those people, that they were mine and I theirs, and that we could not be alien to one another even though we were total strangers. It was like waking from a dream of separateness, of spurious self-isolation in a special world, the world of renunciation and supposed holiness. The whole illusion of a separate holy existence is a dream. Not that I question the reality of my vocation or of my monastic life: but the conception of "separation from the world" that we have in the monastery too easily presents itself as a complete illusion: the illusion that by making vows we become a different species of being: pseudo-angels, "spiritual men", men of interior life, what have you.
>
> Certainly these traditional values are very real, but their reality is not of an order outside everyday existence in a contingent world, nor does it entitle one to despise the secular: though "out of the world" we are in the same world as everybody else, the world of the bomb, the world of race-hatred, the world of technology, the world of mass media, big business, revolution, and all the rest. We take a different attitude to all these things for we belong to God. And yet, so does everybody else belong to God. We just happen to be conscious of it, and to make a profession out of this consciousness. But does that entitle us to consider ourselves different or even *better* than the others? The whole idea is preposterous!

This sense of liberation from an illusory difference was such a relief and such a joy to me that I almost laughed out loud. And I suppose my happiness could have taken form in the words, "Thank God, thank God that I am like other men, that I am only a man among others". To think that for sixteen or seventeen years I had been taking seriously this pure illusion that is implicit in so much of our monastic thinking....

This changes nothing in the sense and value of my solitude, for it is in fact the function of solitude to make one realize such things with a clarity that would be impossible to anyone completely immersed in the other cares, the other illusions, and all the automatisms of a tightly collective existence. My solitude, however, is not my own for I see now how much of it belongs to them—and that I have a responsibility for it in their regard, not just in my own. It is because I am one with them that I owe it to them to be alone, and when I am alone they are not "they" but my own self. There are no strangers.

This feeling became so strong in the early 1960s that by the time *Seeds of Destruction* was published in 1964, Merton knew that in a time when language was compromised, speech imperilled and mutilated by the "amplified noise of beasts," it was time for a monk to speak: loudly, eloquently, unapologetically.

And so, prompted by the moral urgency of the '60s, the silent one broke silence and began to speak out on the pressing social and political issues of the day.

To recover the glory of the human being and to protect the individual in Mammoth Society are titanic tasks, but Merton was determined, with the apocalyptic energy and visionary urgency of a latter-day William Blake, to take them on and to develop for the late 20th century a strategy for spiritual and intellectual coping. To do this effectively, he needed to identify those specific areas that constituted the greatest threat to human wholeness. He found these emblems of political fury to be technology, war and racism.

Merton spoke of technology in terms that first seek to desacralize it, for many have turned it into a surrogate religion, complete with priestly castes, codes of conduct, channels of divine authority, and a working jargon that connotes cosmic benedictions and offers of grace and salvation. What he most deplored was not technology per se but the mentality, the philosophy that undergirds Western culture's subservience to it. It is technologism that is the threat, and technologism is Blake's Urizen. Humanity is prepared to, as Blake phrased it, "bring out number, weight and measure in a year of dearth" and to serve unthinkingly in the "Mills of Satan & Beelzeboul." The rule of technology, then, is the rule of Urizen: subtle, insinuating, comprehensive and insidious. It is also total.

The most demonic expression of technology's capacity to effect human regression to a "climate of moral infancy" is the Adolf Eichmann affair. Spirited away by the Israeli Mossad from his hideout in Argentina in 1960 and tried for his crimes in the Holy Land, Eichmann and his trial, judgment and execution captured the imagination of the world. Hannah Arendt, the philosopher and journalist who covered the trial for the American press, particularly *The New Yorker,* succeeded through her reportage and commentary in rousing passions, accusations, recriminations and a bout of soul-searching not seen since the Nuremburg trials. Merton was transfixed by the trial and its coverage; the Eichmann affair became an obsession, and he wrote about it and its consequences in poetry, diary entry and essay. In Eichmann, totalitarianism and technologism came together in one frightful, satanic symbiosis.

Eichmann was the quintessentially "sane" man who represented the crisis of the liberal conscience and the impotence of a humane tradition in the face of the unspeakable savageries of the Reich. At his trial, the moral bankruptcy of Nazi Germany was condemned, but the European belief in the rule of Reason and the morality of high culture was also judged as wanting.

In Eichmann, Merton saw the immaculate German officer who was also a symbol of the corruption of obedience, the sterility of the Kantian conception of duty, and the wedding of technology with death. In "parodistic and ultimately negating" form, Merton wrote a poem that he describes as lugubrious, a florilegium of bureaucratic and official statements and documents that render the impact of the poem devastating in its moral outrage.

This 1961 Swiftian prose poem "Chant to be Used in Processions Around a Site with Furnaces" is an emblem of the totalitarianism that follows upon the death of private conscience and the triumph of the collectivity.

The poem is structured as a dramatic monologue. The speaker, an unnamed commander of a concentration camp of which Eichmann is the *type*, justifies his life's work—implementing the Final Solution—*after* he has been executed. Defending himself, he protests that

> In my days we worked hard we saw what we did our self sacrifice was conscientious and complete our work was faultless and detailed

There is no compunction, no suggestion even of doubt as the commandant works diligently to improve operations:

> I was the commander I made improvements and installed a guaranteed system taking account of human weakness I purified and I remained decent
>
> How I commanded

The speaker is proud of what he has accomplished because he knows that he cannot be faulted as an officer—"All the while I had obeyed perfectly"—and his final justification is the unsettling accusation against those who witness his execution:

> You smile at my career but you would do as I did if you knew
> yourself and dared

The moral vacuity of the commandant is accompanied by an extraordinary rectitude of manner and conviction, revealing the gaping insufficiency of an abstract morality. The Eichmann affair demands "existential respect for the human reality" at the same time as it underscores the inhumanity of an individual who represents the ideal incarnation of rationality, unaffected by feeling and conscience, the perfect automaton for the millennium. Eichmann is *the* technologistic person: sane, efficient, loyal and a harbinger of death. In his bitterly ironic essay, "A Devout Meditation in Memory of Adolf Eichmann," Merton denounces a notion of sanity shorn of its spiritual moorings, a notion of sanity stripped of justice, love and compassion.

In the hands of Eichmann and his breed, technology became death's most productive associate, language was compromised, values uprooted, human meaning gutted.

Merton abhorred all forms of totalitarianism, a term that he defined very broadly. He once said that if he hadn't joined a monastery, he would surely have been an anarchist politically, for he could not abide any institution that exerted its will over human beings. He expressed his loathing of totalitarianism vividly in the prologue to *The Living Bread*, where he deplored the totalitarian instinct to degrade others, manipulate the truth in the service of power, and prioritize political opportunism over human integrity. Everything is advanced in the interests of manufacturing a lie, the lie that subjects, defiles and even extinguishes the other.

Such a lie is false freedom. But the theme of Merton's life was his quest for real freedom. By the time he wrote *Conjectures of a Guilty Bystander*, Merton was able to articulate what this freedom meant to him:

> Freedom from domination, freedom to live one's own spiritual life, freedom to seek the highest truth, unabashed by any human pressure or any collective demand, the ability to say one's own *yes* and one's own *no*, and not merely to echo the *yes* and the *no* of state, party, corporation, army, or system. This is inseparable from an authentic religion.

Influenced by George Orwell and Aldous Huxley, Merton identified totalitarianism with communist states or dictatorships, but it was certainly not restricted to these. In *Seeds of Destruction* he said that we find traces of totalitarianism in various contexts—contexts that are

> religious or otherwise, from Calvin to Stalin, from Port Royal to Hitler, there are traces of it in Plato and Saint Augustine. We see it in the Fathers of the Church like Tertullian; it provides specious reasons for the Inquisition, as well as for Auschwitz.

In his search for real freedom, Merton was influenced by Erich Fromm, psychoanalyst, humanist and author of such books as *Escape from Freedom* and *The Sane Society*. The two men became friends and shared their ideas by correspondence. William Graf, an American Catholic theologian and priest, has long studied the relationship between the two:

> The common interest in the survival of the human race in its struggle for freedom was the bond that cemented the relationship of these two monks. Both expressed an urgency for their reading audience to respond in some concrete fashion or at least become aware of the loss of freedom that they

were suffering under governments and societies based on a technology and an advertising scheme, and we might call it at times propaganda, that informed them as they sat passively open-mouthed before the TV sets what they needed to be happy but not necessarily free.

Recognizing that they were prophets often speaking into deaf ears, Merton and Fromm found in each other a willing listener and a strong support. They are prophets who challenge eloquently and passionately those institutions which promised happiness rather than freedom. Merton says that the most important question that we can ask is not Am I happy? but Am I free?

Merton frequently wrote about the false freedom based on an illusory happiness.

In order to rid ourselves of the false values and general complacency characteristic of our era, Merton felt that we must cleanse the enormous mass of mental and emotional rubbish that clutters our minds. Without this housecleaning, he told us, we cannot begin to see, and unless we see, we cannot think. This cleansing should begin, said Merton, with the mass media. He deplored the superficiality, reductionist tendencies, easy trivialization and blatant misrepresentations that defined the content of most consumer magazines, newspapers and television fare. In the end, media that is indifferent to human dignity, plays frivolously with the truth and prioritizes sales over substance and critique diminishes us all.

So Merton wrote of a new society that would be radically different from the present one, a society in which the human would no longer be diminished, and would be actively and freely involved in the world. Such a society will value the labour of all, be equitable and participate in the Kingdom of God by means of justice and mercy. In other words, the new society will be a society grounded in divine truth. Although Merton was not a Marxist or a utopian, he did accept some of the Marxist critique of our social and economic order.

While Merton accepted some of the basic tenets of Marx, he thought that Marxist societies were guilty of emphasizing the economic condition at the expense of the human. He also deplored the Marxist endorsement of violence as a means of achieving social change. Rather, he saw Christian education, the teaching of love and truth, as the way and means of realizing the new society. Merton spoke of Marxism and monasticism in his final talk at Bangkok, delivered just hours before his death:

> The difference between the monk and the Marxist is funda-
> mental insofar as the Marxist view of change is oriented to the
> change of economic substructures and the monk is seeking
> to change man's consciousness. Permit me then to spell this
> out a little bit for the information of those who have not been
> meditating on Marxism recently, and who haven't really done
> much homework on Marxism, which I think would be important
> for monks. So the basic approach to reality which the Marxist
> takes is that if you want to understand man's predicament in
> the world, you have to understand the economic processes by
> which he makes his living. And if you fail to understand these
> processes, no matter how good your explanations and answers
> may be, they are wide of the mark. Because ignoring this basic
> economic substructure, they build something that has no valid-
> ity on a different approach which ignores this economic starting
> point and becomes what they call a mystification.
>
> In these terms, therefore, for Marxism, you have three
> great sources of mystification, which are religion, philosophy
> and politics. Religion and philosophy and politics ignore the
> economic basis of man's being and so forth and so therefore are
> wide of the mark. All right. Now I don't want to go any further

on that, it is just enough to give you some idea of what Marxism says, and it of course is very insufficient.

Traditional monasticism faces the same problem of man and his happiness and what his life is for, and approaches it from a different angle. Buddhist and Christian monasticism start from the problem inside man himself. Instead of dealing with the external structures of society, they start with man's own consciousness. And both Christianity and Buddhism agree that the root of man's problems is that his consciousness is all fouled up, and that he does not apprehend reality as it fully and really is. That the moment he looks at something he begins to interpret it in ways which are prejudiced and predetermined to fit a certain wrong picture of the world in which he is as an individual ego in the centre of things.

Christianity and Buddhism alike seek to bring about a transformation in man's consciousness, and instead of starting with matter itself and moving up to a new structure in which man will automatically develop a new consciousness, the traditional religions begin with the consciousness of the individual, seek to transform and liberate the truth in each person with the idea that it will then communicate itself to others. And of course the man par excellence to whom this task is deputed is the monk. The monk is a man who has attained or is about to attain or seeks to attain full realization. And he dwells in the centre of society as one who has attained realization. He knows the score. He has come to experience the grounds of his own being in such a way that he knows the secret of liberation and can somehow or other communicate this to others.

Merton's vision of the new society was by no means a simple one, and he was deeply aware of the social problems that must be solved before such a society could be possible. Consequently, much of his writing during the '60s was devoted to the more immediate issues of the time: racism, war and nuclear destruction. Merton became interested in the problem of the African American well before the 1960s. Before he entered Gethsemani, he worked briefly at a settlement house in New York's Harlem, where he experienced directly the horrible manifestations of racism. He wrote of the impact of this experience in his autobiography, *The Seven Storey Mountain.*

> Here in this huge, dark, steaming slum, hundreds of thousands of Negros are herded together like cattle, most of them with nothing to eat and nothing to do. All the senses and imagination and sensibilities and emotions and sorrows and desires and hopes and ideas of a race with vivid feelings and deep emotional reactions are forced in on upon themselves, bound inward by an iron ring of frustration: the prejudice that hems them in with its four insurmountable walls. In this huge cauldron inestimable natural gifts, wisdom, love, music, science, poetry are stamped down and left to boil with the dregs of an elementally corrupted nature, and thousands upon thousands of souls are destroyed by vice and misery and degradation, obliterated, wiped out, washed from the register of the living, dehumanized.
>
> What has not been devoured in your dark furnace, Harlem? By marijuana, by gin, by insanity, hysteria, syphilis?
>
> Those who manage somehow to swim to the top of the seething cauldron, and remain on its surface, through some special spiritual quality or other or because they've been able to get away from Harlem and go to some college or school, these are not all at once annihilated: but they are left with the dubious privilege of living out the only thing that Harlem possesses in the way of an ideal. They are left with the sorry task of contemplating and imitating what passes for culture in the world of the White people.

Now the terrifying paradox of the whole thing is this: Harlem itself, and every individual in it, is a living condemnation of our so-called culture. Harlem is there by way of a divine indictment against New York City, and the people who live downtown and make their money downtown. The brothels of Harlem, and all its prostitution, and its dope-rings, and all the rest are the mirror of the polite divorces and the manifold cultured adulteries of Park Avenue: they are God's commentary on the whole of our society.

Harlem is, in a sense, what God thinks of Hollywood, and Hollywood is all Harlem has, in its despair, to grasp at by way of a surrogate for heaven.

With this background, Merton followed the civil rights campaigns of the '60s with more than a moralist's interest. His friendships with James Baldwin, Eldridge Cleaver—whose book *Soul on Ice* pays homage to him—and Martin Luther King, who was slated to visit Gethsemani on the very trip that ended with his assassination in Memphis, attests to both the esteem and the confidence he enjoyed among the leaders of the racial struggle. It was King particularly, and his doctrine of non-violence, that most influenced Merton. And here Merton speaks sadly of the irony of King's death in the following excerpt from one of his recorded sessions with his novices:

First of all, this question of the death of Martin Luther King is a little closer to home than you realize. Because, maybe you know this, I don't know, maybe you do, but you don't know the details. Some mutual friends of his and mine in Atlanta were discussing with Martin Luther King about his coming here for a retreat in preparation for the March on Washington. And one of the times when he could have come was last week, this last week, and they were sort of thinking about it. And I got this letter from this Quaker woman in Atlanta written on Wednesday, which was the day that Martin Luther King went to Memphis, so I'll just read what she says.

"Wednesday: Martin is going to Memphis today and I learned (there are some change of plans) he won't be back until the weekend, so John will see him next week (see, her husband was going to talk to him tomorrow and get another plan going). If the Memphis march becomes violent again, there will be a terrible shattering for him. I hope both he and Nhất Hạnh will soon go to Gethsemani. (Nhất Hạnh is this Buddhist from Viet Nam.) If Martin had taken a period there (at Gethsemani) he might have had the wisdom in repose to stay out of Memphis in the first place. And it was a mistake to go there. He had done no preparation and came in cold to a hot situation where the young militants had him just where they wanted him" (so forth and so forth).

So, in other words, it was kind of a crucial and sort of providential thing. He might have come here. And if he had come here he wouldn't have gone to Memphis, and if he hadn't gone to Memphis he wouldn't have got killed. The thing is, too, one of the things you have to understand is that this whole race situation is much more complicated right now than it looks to us, because there is a big division within the Negro people themselves. See most of the Negro people don't want this violence and they are trying to keep this thing non-violent and trying to keep the thing quiet. And you've got a lot of young kids who are very mad and very fanatical. Some of them are members of certain movements and others aren't. And they are trying to push the violence. See? And he was actually caught between those two groups in Memphis, and that was one of the things that made the thing so tough for him. What he was trying to do was keep the whole thing non-violent.

Thanks to King, Merton began to see the moral and political validity of a non-violent movement aimed at converting the opponent and benefiting him by releasing him from his sense of guilt. A movement oriented ultimately towards healing the sin of racism.

Though a central figure in the civil rights movement, Merton would not allow his involvement with it to eclipse other more global issues, such as war and nuclear disarmament, more particularly the Viet Nam War. On this issue, the influence of both Mahatma Gandhi and Origen is marked. Gordon Zahn, the distinguished Catholic sociologist and pacifist, recounts his frank and intricate reading of Merton on the endlessly imperative but vexatious issues around peace:

> The public image of the cloistered Trappist, sworn to silence and self-imposed exile from the world and its affairs, was shattered by the emergence of *this* Trappist, who dared to speak out on the most controversial issue of the day. Not only that: what he had to say was obviously based upon a mastery of facts and their implications far superior to that achieved by the presumably better informed and more experienced citizen outside in the world. It is no surprise that many of the latter thought it unseemly, if not improper, for a contemplative monk to engage in public controversy, a judgment shared by some of his Trappist brethren and superiors as well. Those of us who did refuse to support World War II and who, once that war was over, continued our feeble witness for peace were generally regarded by mainstream Catholics as a kind of lunatic fringe, if not guilty of downright heresy. It was precisely this lack of previous identification, with our suspect ideas and activities, that contributed to the tremendous impact Merton's entry into the debate over the morality of nuclear war would have.

Although Merton certainly stressed pacifism, he disavowed what he called the purely pacifist rejection of war. Zahn continues:

> He rejected pacifism as the term is generally understood. Indeed, he does not even seem to have been a nuclear pacifist, rejecting all possibility of the just use of such weapons. But more must be said. It is equally clear from the overall thrust of his writings that his heart was with the pacifists. However much allowance he might make *in theory* to the traditional just war teachings, his rejection of war *in fact* was no less definite or thorough than that of the pure pacifism he so studiously disclaimed.
>
> Indeed, if we examine Merton's writings and his actions, there is no doubt that he strongly supported passive resistance at least by the 1960s. Thus for Merton, the only objective to be sought by the way of protest is truth and the mutual discovery and sharing of that truth by the practitioner of non-violence and his adversary. His big contribution to the Catholic Peace Movement was to make it respectable. During the war and after the war, I guess those of us who were conscientious objectors, people like Dorothy Day, too, would have been written off, for the most part, as part of the lunatic fringe.
>
> But then all of a sudden, here is this great spiritual writer and contemplative coming out and denouncing nuclear war. And something like that must have been a shock to many of the people. I know it was a shock to his community. So he made us respectable. Then he drew more and more people into this interest, and what has been called the great Catholic peace conspiracy, the Berrigan brothers' [Phil and Dan] activities, and so forth, in a sense may have had their beginning at Gethsemani, because in 1964 he conducted a retreat on the spiritual roots of protest. And I think with the exception of only two or three of the highly select group that attended, all of them went to prison

for one act of resistance or other later on. The two Berrigans were there, and two other people who were involved in I think the Milwaukee and the Catonsville raids, and then Tom Cornell was there who later burned his draft card.

He opposed the draft card burnings. He made that quite clear in one of his articles, in that he felt that it confused the communication, that it made people who were already kind of fearful of the peace movement more fearful, because of the radical nature of it, and also I guess it scandalized people to have folk burn their draft cards. As far as the raids are concerned, he had reservations about them. He said he felt that they came to the edge of violence and that if ever the peace movement escalated into violence it would be escalating into self-contradiction.

But he didn't say that he felt that the Catonsville raid was that, he just had misgivings. The only thing that he really objected to—and he objected strongly; he immediately withdrew his name from peace associations that he had been involved in, but fortunately just for a short time, he came right back again—was when this young Catholic Worker burned himself in protest against the war. He felt, I guess, some sort of responsibility; if the Catholic peace movement was going into such extremism, he didn't want to have anything to do with it. But he was convinced later on by people that this really wasn't a Catholic peace movement action, it was an individual action that this fellow had taken.

As a result of Merton's outspoken stands on decidedly public issues, he found himself in conflict with some of the senior officials of the Church, and for a period of time he was forbidden to publish anything of a delicate political nature. Biographer John Howard Griffin offers some insight into how Merton handled this situation:

The whole implication of that refusal was that a Trappist monk should be praying and meditating and not concerning himself with these worldly matters. When Pope John XXIII published his encyclical called *Pacem in Terris*, Merton, who never was really ever subdued, bounced back from his humiliating censure and wrote to the General, "I suppose it's really fortunate that the Holy Father didn't have you as his censor, because he's published in *Pacem in Terris* the very same things that I've been saying all these years and you haven't let me publish, so now that he's said them how about letting me publish?"

As well as relying on his sense of humour, Merton coped with this censorship not by leaving the Church, as some did, and not even, strictly, by disobedience, but by protesting against it in his own way. He wrote a large correspondence, now aptly called the *Cold War Letters*. Gordon Zahn explains:

For this time, when Merton was not supposed to be publishing things on war and so forth, he circulated a gathering of letters that he had written, which didn't deal only with war, they dealt with all sorts of social issues: again racism, and all this. They were to prominent people, and also small people. I remember the fascinating thing about it [being] just identified by the initials, and you tried to figure out who they were. I figured out some of them: Erich Fromm was one and Karl Stern, another psychiatrist. I think Eunice Kennedy was one, and all this type of thing. So he had this great range: Dorothy Day, several exchanges of letters with DD. And in that he was sort of carrying on a special ministry of social concern.

This was again astonishing for someone who supposedly was behind monastery walls, working away in the monastery garden, or something like that, and there he was in a sense reaching people, many people of influence but also many people who apparently just read his books and asked his advice or commented.

The Cold War letters underscore this. They were mimeographed—apparently, he was able to send mimeograph stuff—and he put them all together and sent them off and he said this is what I'll do now, and maybe the time will come when I have to write on backs of envelopes, but he was going to keep doing it. It was obedience that he did not fight against the silencing rule, but he made use of whatever loopholes or permissions were incorporated in that to get the message out.

And so from the seclusion of a quite unmodern institution, Merton addressed himself to the modern issues of the day. Ever watchful of Armageddon, Merton feared the amassing armies of the night, and warned a callous age of its imminent ruin.

Merton:

A day of ominous decision has now dawned on this free nation.
Armed with a titanic weapon, and convinced of our own right,
We face a powerful adversary, armed with the same weapon,
　　　equally convinced that he is right....

In this fatal moment of choice in which we might begin the
　　　patient architecture of peace
We may also take the last step across the rim of chaos.

Save us then from our obsessions! Open our eyes, dissipate our
　　　confusions,
teach us to understand ourselves and our adversary! ...

Grant us prudence in proportion to our power,
Wisdom in proportion to our science,
Humaneness in proportion to our wealth and might.
And bless our earnest will to help all races and peoples to
　　　travel, in friendship with us,
Along the road to justice, liberty and lasting peace: ...

Grant us to see your face in the lightning of this cosmic storm,
O God of holiness, merciful to men:
Grant us to seek peace where it is truly found!

In your will, O God, is our peace!

Amen

4

Merton's Religious Imagination

THOMAS MERTON WAS in many ways the foremost religious figure of the mid-20th century. His religious books, meditations, primers of the spiritual life for the novice and the seasoned, essays on the contemplative life for the laity and many others created for Merton, by the time of his death, a remarkable readership that would be the envy of any bestselling writer. His religious books particularly were published in many languages and underwent many printings. He was, in the worldly sense of the term, a success. The world has never quite got over the phenomenal popularity of a man who quite emphatically rejected its ways. Having retreated into the woods to a strict cloister, Merton continued his commerce with humanity, a commerce that revealed a depth of insight and rare perspective that only his withdrawal could actually provide.

Eager to remind the world of the folly and despair of its frenzied ways, the Monk of Kentucky, who called himself the guilty bystander, never ceased to warn a recalcitrant age. He became the silent witness to an inner truth that too few acknowledged; he continued his books and pamphlets, letters and poems so that none could say of him that he cared not a whit for the world. His incredible productivity is but one measure of the man's charisma—the unequivocal sign of his renown. Again and again, he wrote so that his readers would listen to the silent-speaking words of their souls and commune with a reality that spoke the quiet sounds of truth. The Monk of the Hills addressed himself to the whirling masses of the city in a language of common concern and searing sincerity.

The monastery of Our Lady of Gethsemani in Kentucky was Merton's home. It was a place of seclusion, serenity, security and solace. He saw the monks as a genuine family, defined by their simplicity, harmony and solitude. For Merton—many years displaced, deprived early in his life of his parents, wandering from one continent to another, unsure of his future, insecure in his relationships—Gethsemani offered stability, peace, order and rhythm. His first decade in the monastery was distinguished by his fervour for the place and his uncritical approach to monastic life. He was still the romantic dreamer.

From the beginning, Merton touched the hearts and imaginations of a growing multitude with his autobiography, *The Seven Storey Mountain*, inspiring large numbers of individuals to seek in the confines of the monastery a truth the outside world could not offer. Books on spirituality poured out of him, appealing to his growing fan club, enticing countless others to read his work, interspersing their release with other books—volumes of verse, a play, social commentaries, advocacy work on behalf of peace, and more—but his bread and butter was his books on the spiritual life. These titles included *No Man Is an Island, The Living Bread, Thoughts in Solitude, Seeds of Contemplation, The Silent Life, New Seeds of Contemplation, Seasons of Celebration* and *The New Man*.

In all his books on the spiritual life, one can find an emphasis on freedom, choice, openness, vulnerability, personhood and integrity. Ever conscious of the forces that conspire against man's freedom—the machinery of totalitarian government, the spirit of mass man, the very dread of Kafka, Jung and Marcel, the light discipline of conformism, the enervating ennui that allows the most horrid compromise, and the ready submission to authority, no matter what its source—Merton saw in contemplation a means of preserving human integrity. He saw the contemplative as more than a sedentary recluse absorbed in his own interiority. Rather, he saw the contemplative as a seeker, a quester, yearning for wholeness, for purity, for depth of meaning. Contemplation is a rare if not occasionally opaque intuition of that God, the *deus absconditus,* or hidden God who is at the heart of all mystical desiring.

Merton's understanding of contemplation itself would undergo various creative mutations. In fact, contemplation came to have multivalent meanings. Initially, the life of a monk necessitates not only a withdrawal from the world but a concomitant spurning of the world's claim on his sympathies. Such a world-hating attitude can easily lead the monk to see the contemplative calling as the most exalted of human endeavours, with its very clear and righteous repudiation of the allurements of all that the flesh can offer. And then some.

Although in his early life as a monk Merton shared this view, it never had a complete hold on him. Eventually, after years of meditation and spiritual growth, he came to see the contemplative life as a *dependence* on God, a dependence organized in such a way that God is both the nexus and the guiding spirit of the individual's life. It is possible, Merton concluded, to be a contemplative outside the cloister.

This is the first of three meanings Merton attached to contemplation: *the spiritual/vocational.* But contemplation in its second meaning for Merton is nothing less than the remaining guarantor of human freedom. The free person, the genuine contemplative, is in harmony with the order of creation, undeceived by public wisdom, alert to the real threats to society.

Contemplation, then, seen as the guarantor of human freedom, is not just a metaphysical proposition. It is a political one as well. Indeed, for Merton, contemplation became his only political article of faith. Not an ideologue by temperament and continually suspicious of all political platforms, Merton discovered in contemplation the only remaining measure that could secure human freedom in an environment of unsympathetic and destructive forces. Even in the peak years of his political awakening—the 1960s—Merton the anarchist, the subversive voice of his novel *My Argument with the Gestapo*, was never far away.

In 1968, Merton would go so far as to argue that the monk, the contemplative par excellence, is engaged in an activity not unlike that of the Marxist revolutionary. Though he stands in judgment, like the Marxist, on the alienating forces of society, the monk is loath to use those means—guerrilla warfare, kidnappings and sabotage—that are too common a feature of revolutionary resistance. The monk seeks liberation from the restrictive and archaic structures of society in order to liberate people from their own self-oppression.

Contemplation's third meaning consists of the means of recovering silence—the final assurance of artistic and spiritual openness. Although it is often cast as art's formidable rival in the arena of perfection, contemplation is vital for artistic integrity.

Theologian William Graf observes of Merton's understanding of freedom the full flowering of contemplation:

> For Merton, the monastery was the school in which he would learn to discover and live the life of freedom; the place in which he would be able to rid himself of the violence of selfishness.

One's true nature, one's real self is found in living rationally and lovingly in the image and likeness of God. The very core of our humanity is God, who is the ultimate freedom. God is the total freedom and participation in the life of God. If one were to renounce or deny the freedom freely given, one would essentially renounce one's very being. The monastic life—and I use this in its broadest context—permits the pilgrim to detach the self from all of those things that the world promises will bring happiness. There comes a time, even within the monastic life, when the very tools which allow for growth in freedom are themselves, however, to be renounced. After the period of alienation, the person becomes aware of the unity with God which is already there; that unity with God which is the true source of reconciliation.

Aware of his own search and his own discoveries, Merton wrote to affect change or, perhaps better, to affect the awareness of the need for change within those structures that allow the person to be alienated and tied to empty promises. The search for union with God, who for Merton is freedom, is natural to us. Freedom is God's gift to humanity. In the fall of 1965, Thomas Merton took up full-time residence in the hermitage on the Gethsemani property. It was a small and basically comfortable place, where there was plenty of silence and inner freedom. And he writes, 'I feel much more human and natural on my own, than when tied up in the routines of an institution. Here I don't have to play my part at all and that is very delightful. I just live.'

As the years pass since his entry into the monastery, Merton found that the degree of solitude and silence that he needed could no longer be secured in his monastic home. For some time he had investigated the role of the anchorite or hermit in the Cistercian tradition and found that precedent had been made and that an Order that emphasized the community aspect of monastic life also allowed for the special gift of the eremitic call. He wished to be a hermit in his own Order. He had longed for the greater solitude that such a life ensures almost from the very beginning of his religious life, and by means of sheer persistence and scholarly endeavour, he finally won his request. Merton became a hermit. In so doing, he recovered and re-established that mode of life that was the true desert vocation. His increased solitude did what he knew it would do—it sharpened his perspective on the world, on the contemplative life, on a life of wholeness and integrity.

Church historian E. Glenn Hinson identifies the models Merton found for his increasing solitude in the monastic environment:

> His models were Clement of Alexandria and Erasmus. Clement was, to him, a model Catholic, in that he articulated the true purpose of culture, a true humanism. According to Merton, the purpose of a Christian humanism should be to liberate man from the mere status of *animalus homo* to at least the level of *rationalis*; not animal, but the rational human, and better still, spiritual or pneumatic. The spiritual person is fully human precisely because he has fulfilled his latent potentiality by life in Spirit that is the Holy Spirit, the Spirit of Christ.
>
> The fact that Merton possessed an unusual ability to commune and communicate beyond words left many to ascribe this to his peculiar genius and personality. And all of those are evident. Those who know Merton's story, however, would never stop there, because Merton himself would not. For they would know his gift was poured, moulded and refined in Merton's own search for community in the Trappist Order. In the last analysis, it was contemplation that equipped him for authentic dialogue and communion with all persons everywhere. Merton's own perception about the uniting role of contemplation is quite visible

in *The Waters of Siloe*, an early writing on the monastic vocation, published in 1949.

"The monk's aim," he noted then, "is love of God, who is love". This love can only be demonstrated by living for the common will, by complete surrender, obedience in every smallest circumstance of the common life. So long as a monk retains private ownership in any corner of his being, he falls short of this union. Contemplation in no way conflicts with the common life, rather it prepares the monk for it; for the more he isolates himself in the will of God, the more he becomes one by charity, with all the others you are united in the same love of God. He treasures solitude and silence, and even physical isolation, so that he may commune with God's spirit, who is the common life of the monastic community and of the whole Church of God. Solitude therefore unites. "The closer the contemplative is to God, the closer he is to others The more he loves God, the more he can love the men he lives with. He does not withdraw from them, shake them off to get away from them, but in the truest sense finds them. *Omnes in Christo unum sumus*." We are all one in Christ. The goal of monasticism is the perfection of the person of Christ, his mystical body.

Merton was schooled in love, freedom and poverty—the Trinitarian basis of the monastic life—an aperture to the mystical life itself. William Graf situates Merton in the Western mystical tradition:

Whether or not Thomas Merton was indeed a mystic will depend on one's own definition of the word. From what he prescribes for his students in a series of weekly conferences given in the 1950s, one can conclude that Merton had vowed himself to a life that would allow for mystical prayer and perhaps mystical prayer experiences. Lecturing to the professed monks, Merton reminds them that they are called to live their theology.

Since without mysticism there is no real theology and without theology there is no mysticism, Merton would require more than just the external and passive observance of the rule. He says, "More is required; we must live our theology—fully, deeply—in its totality. Without that, there is no sanctity."

At least Merton, we could agree, falls within the general definition that the oft-quoted Evelyn Underhill gives: mysticism is the art of unity with reality. The mystic is a person who has attained that union in greater or lesser degree, or who at least aims at and believes in such attainment. As he sat before the monks and the religious gathered at Bangkok, around the 27th anniversary of his arrival at Gethsemani, towards the conclusion of his lecture, the pilgrim Merton best expressed what he had been searching for from January 31st, 1915, until his death on that fateful 10th day of December in 1968:

If you once penetrate by detachment and purity of heart to the inner secret of the ground of your ordinary experience, you attain to a liberty that nobody can touch, that nobody can affect, that no political change of circumstances can do anything to.

Determined to reclaim contemplation and mysticism for all men and women and to eliminate the notion that considers contemplation the prerogative of the clergy, Merton wrote handbooks for the spiritual life for modern men and women; those who wish to become lay contemplatives. For them, there is no claustral retreat; their cell can be found amid the highrise and the slum.

Lay theologian Kenneth Russell assessed Merton's contributions to an expansive and inclusive understanding of contemplation:

I can remember in 1949 when Thomas Merton's *Seeds of Contemplation* came out. I was a teenager and I can remember one of the great things in my life was picking up that volume. Merton recognized that there are lay people who are called to a properly contemplative life. In fact, he tells us in *The Seven Storey Mountain* that there was one period, if we remember, that he thought that no religious order was going to have him. The Franciscans didn't want him and he thought his religious career had come to an end.

But at that point he decided to live as a contemplative in the world. In *Seeds of Contemplation*, Thomas Merton offers advice to contemplatives in the world; he counsels them to push back the noise and distractions of society and to take refuge in some corner or room where they can be undisturbed. He advises them to try and work out-of-doors, in some job that will not rattle their peace. But beyond this, there are few specific suggestions.

In one section of the unpublished manuscript of *The Inner Experience*, Merton does make some proposals. Those desiring to live a contemplative life must, first of all, lessen their contact with the world as much as possible, by reducing their need for pleasure, comfort, prestige and success. Then they must learn to put up with the conflict that remains—the noise, the pressures, the secular mentality that is everywhere. When he comes to specific suggestions for lay contemplatives, he focuses on the problem of making space for prayer and quiet in a busy world. He advises the contemplative to make use of the parts of the day the world does not value, such as the early hours of the morning—very little is going on at three or four. He advises them to keep Sunday as the special day of light it was meant to be. He wonders if it would not be wise to move to the country or a small town in order to enjoy a slower pace of life and the time for thought that comes with it. He also advises contemplatives to form small prayer groups to support and encourage one another.

A contemplative, then, for Merton is no different from others, but understands the problems of existence–their physical and spiritual origins–not through means of analysis but by means of simplicity.

Russell understands that Merton's broad view

> ... of the contemplative life reaches out to include lay people who feel called to centre their lives quietly on meditation and prayer. Because of his deep understanding of the nature of prayer, and because he is able to reshape spiritual tradition to both the psychological and sociological realities of our time, Merton serves as a real guide to lay contemplatives. His explicit statements on the contemplative life outside the cloister confirm and justify the pull some of the laity feel toward orienting their lives toward prayer and quiet.
>
> But if we want to fully appreciate Merton's contribution, we must realize that when he grasped the notion that the solitary does not necessarily imply a monk at all, he arrived at a deinstitutionalized notion of the contemplative person which eliminates the old danger of imposing a monastic spirituality and monastic values on lay contemplatives. By reducing in his writings and witness the clash of apparently conflicting obligations to the question of what is appropriate to each person's particular role and circumstances, Merton offers contemplatives, meditators, irrespective of their lifestyle or vocation, sound guidance for the interior life amidst the spiritual hustle and bustle and straining realities of their existence.

The quintessential monk, Merton was more Catholic than any narrow definition of that term could suggest. His monasticism, the very core of his Catholicism, was a rich ecumenical undertaking that paid no heed to the strictures of sect, time or mortality. He was a monk for all and for all seasons. As he says in *Conjectures of a Guilty Bystander*:

The more I am able to affirm others, to say "yes" to them in myself, by discovering them in myself and myself in them, the more real I am. I am fully real if my own heart says *yes* to *everyone*. I will be a better Catholic, not if I can refute every shade of Protestantism, but if I can affirm the truth in it and still go further.

So, too, with the Muslims, the Hindus, the Buddhists, etc. This does not mean syncretism, indifferentism, the vapid and careless friendliness that accepts everything by thinking of nothing. There is much that one cannot "affirm" and "accept", but first, one must say yes where one really can.

If I affirm myself as a Catholic merely by denying all that is Muslim, Jewish, Protestant, Hindu, Buddhist, etc., in the end I will find that there is not much left for me to affirm as a Catholic: and certainly no breath of the Spirit with which to affirm it.

Merton had a special affinity to the mystical in Judaism and Islam. Edward Kaplan is the official biographer of the Jewish theologian and mystic Abraham Joshua Heschel, a spiritual figure with whom Merton had many similarities:

Thomas Merton and Abraham Heschel, both born in Europe, matured and fulfilled their missions in the United States, motivated by a similar love for their adopted homeland combined with a militant spiritual criticism. In contrast to most members of their orthodox communities, they harmonized personal piety and radical moral involvement. Merton expressed his modified pacifism and progressive social views in numerous articles and speeches. Heschel also strongly opposed the Viet Nam War and marched beside Martin Luther King during the Selma-Montgomery protest. Both started their professional careers as proponents of mysticism and both were poets who savoured language and the richness of the imagination. Both speak to our opposing demands of history and tranquility, our anger at or love for God, and they questioned the very foundations of religion in our time.

Heschel and Merton, as Jew and Christian, understood human callousness as alienation from God. Both accompanied their readers to the terrifying depths of their loneliness while nurturing a sense of divine Presence which all people can share. Prayer, for both, plumbs the abyss of humanity and places us before God as responsible persons. Prayer is their touchstone of truth. They stood firmly before God and spoke to the world, and to their co-religionists, with a spiritually radical conscience.

They judged society and religious institutions alike by God's standards and so realized the partnership of Judaism and Christianity in a troubled world. To society they voiced the demands of divine justice and compassion against the forces of warfare, social and economic oppression and indifference. They challenged the self-interested withdrawal fostered by religious institutionalism. Heschel sought to balance the traditional Jewish emphasis on external observance, or *halakha*, with the inner life of devotion, *agada*. He believed ethnicity less essential to Judaism than relationship with the living God; impassioned prayer, not ethical culture, should foster a burning prophetic concern. Merton deplored the unreflective traditionalism of the American Catholic hierarchy. He sought to liberate the inner person: a mystical relationship with God which would abolish the defensive self-centeredness that inhibits moral courage. Contemplatives, who specialized in devotion and personal authenticity, could become prophetic witnesses.

Their militant devotion to the divine image of humanity remains a beacon in our dark night as an anguished and floundering world. Merton and Heschel disagreed on creeds and commitments at the heart of their respective traditions. But they were firmly united in their anxiety before humanity and God. They were faithful visionaries.

For William Nicholls, the Anglican priest and a fellow graduate of Clare College, Merton the interreligious model par excellence was in various parts contemplative, monk and theologian:

> Merton had a great deal to say to what is going on right now in the parishes: the very strong polarization in every church and every parish between the traditionalists and the radicals. And the traditionalists who want to hold on to and relate to the theologies of the past and the liturgical patterns that have been inherited and, perhaps, a certain triumphalism of the past, which is very hard to sustain. And the radicals who want to revise everything—change the theology, change the liturgy—until it becomes a kind of group rap session. They get very involved in all forms of social action.
>
> Merton doesn't seem to be quite on either side of that conflict. He says so rather clearly, I think, as a matter of fact, in one of his essays, *Contemplation in a World of Action*. That what the Church has to bring to the modern world, he thought, and I think this might prove to be a very fruitful insight, is not adaptation and relevance, simply, but bringing in the substance of its own spiritual tradition into relevance in the modern world, and had the churches been doing that, some might think they may not have been in the position they now are.
>
> So Merton might turn out to be not at all a theoretical concern, but the most practical concern to the parish priest and the pastor, wherever he may be. A very helpful point, I think, was made by someone who said that it is important to see that Merton really was a theologian—that a theologian is not necessarily a person with no feelings, that Merton's thought was permeated by love; it was a felt theology and that's what theology ought to be like. If there is to be theology, it should be of that sort.

Not all people think of Merton as a theologian, however. Anglican theologian Donald Grayston makes it clear:

Let's agree that Merton was never a theologian in any systematic sense. And he would of course agree with that claim because he made it himself, but that only after he had written that awful book *The Ascent to Truth*, where he had tried to be a scholastic theologian and failed totally and utterly. But that was partly due to his sense of loyalty to the institution of the Roman Catholic Church. He felt that in order to be a loyal Roman Catholic, you had be a scholastic and you had to be all in favour of Saint John of the Cross and really that's all you could do was work in those categories.

Merton is best classified as a religious thinker in the tradition of Pascal and in the tradition of Simone Weil. I think that really, the best word for Merton is a French one: *savant*. He is a *savant*. I think that word conveys something more than scholar or thinker. He's a thinker, he's a scholar, he's a learned man, he's an erudite man, he's a wise man. In one of the manuscripts of *Seeds of Contemplation*, in a passage that wasn't printed even in the first version, he says something to the effect—after two or three paragraphs of diatribe on contemporary society— well, what can you expect after 500 years of Protestantism, apparently being willing to attribute the spiritual decay of the modern world entirely to Protestantism. And from there to his real respect to Barth and Bonhoeffer in *Conjectures of a Guilty Bystander*—that's really quite a jump.

His denigration of Anglicanism in *The Seven Storey Mountain* was one of the reasons, of course, why the English convert novelist Evelyn Waugh thought it was so great. But from my own point of view as an Anglican priest, I think virtually everything he said about the Anglican Church in *The Seven Storey Mountain* was justified. He went to Zion Church in Douglaston [New York] looking for some religion and found book reviews. He had been to Oakham School as a young teenager and in religion class all he got was lectures on rowing from the chaplain, who rejoiced in the glorious name of Buggy Jerwood. And he pointed out how, in a cultural sense, the Church of England had become so acculturated, that it was part of that great warm glow in the heart of every Englishman, which included Christmas pantomimes, and *The Times* of London, and the Queen going to Sandringham at Christmas, and Father Christmas, and all this kind of thing.

I think there is a marvellous example of his reconciling himself with some of the extreme judgments that he had passed; some of the really intolerant judgments and immature judgments he had passed in *The Seven Storey Mountain*. In his later journals, it's almost as if, in a sense, he was returning to them and setting them right—correcting them, some of these early excesses. He did this with what he calls The English Angels in *Conjectures of a Guilty Bystander*: he goes back and talks about a number of the English traditions that formed him, and he talks about them quite lovingly.

But he does so even more markedly with The French Angels, because in *The Seven Storey Mountain*, the passages he has about French spirituality—about its insipidity and not only the terrors of the Lycée Ingres, at Montauban, but the general appreciation of a high insipid French Catholicism—some really vile passages. He makes amends for it in *Conjectures of a Guilty Bystander* when he talks about the Catholicism of France and the Catholicism that formed him and its great vision, its intensity. Although he makes it quite clear that although he likes Pascal, he still doesn't like Descartes.

What Merton disliked about Descartes and the Cartesian tradition was the reduction of the true self to the thinking 'I'. In contrast to Descartes' *cogito ergo sum*, "I think therefore I am," Merton offered the world mystical and evangelical counsel, "I love therefore I am," and recognized in this the supreme importance of being part of humanity.

Merton's spirituality consisted of a rediscovery of the true or real self that is ultimate freedom—that is God. An authority on Merton's spirituality, William Shannon, outlines Merton's long quest to discover his true or real self:

> This may seem at first sight to be an easy task. In fact, it is an immensely difficult one, for knowing God—which is absolutely necessary in order to know my true self—is not the same thing as knowing *about* God. I have, in my natural being, no capacity to be activated by my own powers that will enable me to know God as God. It is true that I can know something about God's existence and nature through reason but, as Merton says, there is no human and rational way by which I can arrive at that possession of God, whereby one will know oneself in knowing God.
>
> The crucial question is how we find the living God in God's own reality and in that divine reality find oneself. The answer to this most basic question is complicated by the fact that there appear to be two forces at work. First, there is a centrifugal force in our natural being, as it is now constituted, that carries us away from our true identity and therefore away from God. At the same time, there is a centripetal force: we can become once again in God who we really are. The centrifugal force is the influence of original sin that draws us away from our centre into regions of unreality; it propels us to build up a superficial, even illusory, *ego* that is ultimately without substance. The centripetal force, on the other hand, is the power of the Holy Spirit, drawing us to our centre: creating a new self in us, or more correctly, uncovering the true self that in essence was actually there all the time, though unable to be awakened by our natural powers. It is only in response to the call initiated by God that we can really find God.
>
> It should be clear that the journey into the land of contemplation is a long journey, in which we have to begin from where

we are and go to where we should be. But the paradox of the journey is that when we arrive at our destination, we discover that we were there all the time. We just did not know it. In this, Merton echoes the words of one of his favourite poets, T.S. Eliot, who wrote in *The Four Quartets*, "We shall not cease from exploration / And the end of all our exploring / Will be to arrive where we started / And know the place for the first time."

5

Pilgrim to the East

ONE OF MERTON'S dearest friends was Amiya Chakravarty. He situates Merton's travels to the East within the context of his aspirations, scholarship and deep attachment to inter-religious dialogue:

> I often remember how Thomas Merton felt about his journey to his Asian destination. "I'm going home," he wrote in his journal, "to the home I've never been in in this body." From that journey, he never came back home to Gethsemani, his monastery and his spiritual centre. But he had discovered the quality of Asia's and India's meditational life, and in a few months' time, before death overtook him in Bangkok, he prayed and walked and joined with people, in festive moments and in aloneness.
>
> He met some religious leaders, like Swami Lokeswarananda of the Ramakrishna Vedanta order; visited His Holiness the Dalai Lama in North India; stood still and entranced before some great stone sculptures of the Buddha in Ceylon—see the variety of his inspiration. His journal reveals the depths, the range of his perceptions, his wholeness and intense concentration in far and foreign lands. No land indeed was far and foreign, for wherever he was, it belonged to the revelatory truth; he accepted the given and the gift of divine life on earth.

When he was with us in India, for the World Conference on Faiths, one day in Calcutta I found him standing in front of our hotel and he simply said, "I'm looking at everything." And he meant just that: an immense and ceaseless procession of cars, rickshaws, beggars, as well as the daily office crowd moved along the streets; the clouds and kites in the sky strayed into his own seeing and feeling universe. But everything for him, even those things that were hurtful and wrong, were a part of some growing fulfillment. Throughout his life he challenged colour barriers, religious tyranny, economic injustice, took up the cause of suffering minorities and majorities. That morning I saw his patience and his oneness with life in a teeming city.

Merton had developed an interest in the East as early as the 1930s. As a novice master in the '50s and '60s, the Trappist writer immersed himself in the wisdom of Asia. It was an abiding passion. Merton understood, as few religious leaders of our time have done, the special importance of the Eastern mind in its unique apprehension of the Divine. The poetry, sculpture, theology and monasticism of the East provided a complement to the traditions and wisdoms of the West. In his own life, Merton sought to realize that merger: the fusion of East and West that would be a true marriage, admitting the vital differences that obtain between them, but uniting in a special way to celebrate their common source and their common end. Merton's interest in Zen Buddhism grew out of his study of the similarities that exist between Asian and European mystical traditions.

Donald Grayston muses on Merton's discovery of Zen:

He investigated all the Eastern traditions while at Columbia University. But he did so completely on an intellectual level and he had no real personal experience of what they really might mean. But my understanding of it is that during the period he was novice master, that was really his mature period and he began to investigate other religions and to correspond with authors of books about them, and began to correspond with Dr. Suzuki, and in fact in the early 1960s he went to see him in New York City.

And really, his full appreciation of Zen came through Suzuki. But it was a very natural kind of thing for two reasons. He was getting tired of Scholasticism. He was realizing that he would never be a creative scholastic theologian—he felt constricted by the continuous classification of categories within scholasticism and he wanted something beyond that. I think his personality type had a lot to do with that. He was what Jung would have called an introverted intuitive; he really was not a thinking type, in spite of the fact that he could think and write very well.

He had worked as a Thomist, in a kind of exaggerated sense of loyalty, both to the Roman Catholic Church and the monastic institution, and finally, in his 40s, just gave up and recognized himself for what he was—an intuitive and highly literary person. I think *New Seeds of Contemplation*, for example, represents a fusion of the Thomistic and Zen traditions. It was a rejection of the prevailing idea in great chunks of the Roman Catholic Church that this was the *only* way to do theology, the *best* way to do theology or the *required* way to do theology. He found that it had taken him a certain way; he had integrated it. He was not rejecting it—he might have been rejecting some of its drier, more moribund parts—but he moved on armed with his Scholastic background and opened himself really to the possibility of spiritual intuition, beyond a subject-object distinction.

This is best seen in his Zen mystical poetry—emblems of mystical fury—that appeared in his *Emblems of a Season of Fury* (1963), poems that reflect his concentrated years of Zen study and exploration in tightly disciplined and word-spare poetics.

In fact, Merton drew upon his spiritual and intellectual mentor, William Blake, to help validate his reading of Zen.

Blake and Zen alike seek the dismantling of Abstraction's hold on creation with its narrow vision and its constricted spirituality. The "doors of perception" are imaginative and spiritual—for Blake they are one and the same—and poetic skill and mystical intuition must align in a common campaign against the "specious reality" that dominates our minds.

Merton the poet longs to restore the integrity and harmony that once existed before individual consciousness or reflexive ego awareness shattered prelapsarian unity. The poet realizes that the only way humankind can recover paradise is not by ratiocination or systematic inquiry, but by a poetic and mystical identification or co-sympathy with creation, discovering in its mystery the *irrelevance* of the 'I' and the illusoriness of the empirical self. As he says in "O Sweet Irrational Worship,"

> My heart's love
> Bursts with hay and flowers.
> I am a lake of blue air
> In which my own appointed place
> Field and valley
> Stand reflected.

What remains hidden to reason may be known to rapture. This is the language of Zen; this is the wisdom of Zen. As he explains in *Conjectures of a Guilty Bystander*:

> The taste for Zen in the West is in part a healthy reaction of people exasperated with the heritage of four centuries of Cartesianism: the reification of concepts; idolization of the reflexive consciousness, flight from being into verbalism, mathematics, and rationalization. Descartes made a fetish out of the mirror in which self finds itself. Zen shatters it.

In solitude, one can rediscover paradise, as the Desert Fathers and Zen masters prove. To do so, however, requires a divestment of the ego so thorough as to virtually deny its reality; it requires a levelling of the will and a subsuming of all desire into the *one* yearning for wholeness, and it requires the realization of a spiritual vulnerability that places the seeker wholly in the hands of the Other. In short, the seeker must empty himself or herself. To be emptied is to love, for the greatest act of love for the Christian is *kenosis*, the self-emptying love of the crucified Jesus. It is *this* kenotic love that every seeker must attain if solitude is to reveal the innocence and purity of heart that is paradise, as Merton makes clear in his Zen poem "Song: If You Seek…":

> Follow my ways and I will lead you
> To golden-haired suns,
> Logos and music, blameless joys,
> Innocent of questions
> And beyond answers:
> For I, Solitude, am thine own self:
> I, Nothingness, am thy All.
> I, Silence, am thy Amen!

Stripped of all presupposition and reflexive awareness, and completely enveloped in the Other—the Non-Object of the seeker's quest—the emptied subject recovers, in solitude, paradise.

Paradise will forever elude the seeker should it be desired, for desire presupposes an object to be possessed. Desire's fulfillment rests in the acquisition of the object desired. The logic of Zen and of the Christian mystics necessitates, however, the dispossession of desire or the death of the ego if the seeker is to be in turn possessed by paradise.

With the language of Zen, a language of extrarational meaning, contradiction and negation, and with the language of Blake, a language of innocence, private mythology and mystical symbol, Merton sought to unveil paradise in the undefiled vision of emptiness.

Zen, he affirmed, allows us to see the vital need for "irrational worship" and the unreasonableness of rationality, when he writes in *Zen and the Birds of Appetite* that the

> point is that facts are not just plain facts. There is a dimension where the bottom drops out of the world of factuality and of the ordinary. Western industrial culture is in the curious position of having simultaneously reached the climax of an entire totalitarian rationality of organization and of complete absurdity and self-contradiction. Existentialists and a few others have noticed the absurdity [Merton was thinking specifically of Albert Camus, on whom he wrote extensively]. But the majority persist in seeing only the rational machinery against which no protest avails: because, after all, it is 'rational,' and it is 'a fact.' So, too, is the internal contradiction . . . It might be good to open our eyes and *see*.

Zen enables Merton to see; it was his means of intersection with memory, innocence and eternity. Zen allowed him to be a child again, to see with fresh eyes, and to taste the mercy of God. But in one sense, as Religious Studies scholar Jacques Goulet has noted, Merton was always the child:

> He's utterly the child. He lives intensely the present moment. For instance, his journal entries consist of many judgments about people and ideas that are full of superlatives. For example, this particular writer is the greatest writer, this thinker the greatest thinker, or the worst. Merton is totally present to the moment at hand. There is no person past or future, just the present with Merton completely in love with you, focused on you, and when he speaks it is to you. He's *your* friend, and when you are gone he

is somebody else's. Now, it has to be admitted, for many people this is disconcerting and they dismiss him as an extremist. But when a child cries, the *whole* person cries, and when a child laughs, the *whole* person laughs. People often demand the adult in Merton and they get the child.

He is too honest to be otherwise.

Take the matter of his Columbia University erotic cartoons, for example, or indeed his relationship with M. We all have a blueprint of someone we consider a saint, the ideal monk, a holy one, and when the idealized person no longer fits the blueprint, either we change our expectations and the blueprint is altered, or we register our disappointment with the idealized figure's failure to meet our specifications. We blame Merton for not con-forming to our mould. We don't allow Merton to be Merton—the perennial child, full of wonder and surprise.

Merton, the Zen child, the Blakean child, not only opened himself to everyone and to every experience with both freshness and a dangerous indifference to caution, he also longed to identify promiscuously with all. The childlike predilection to imaginatively embrace all was never erased with adulthood; it was just transformed into his capacity for universal empathy. Exploring ever deeper those layers of empathy was one of the driving motivations for his trip to the East, a trip that would prove his final pilgrimage, a trip to which theologian and publisher Herbert Richardson attaches great significance:

"This geographical pilgrimage," he said, "is the symbolic acting out of an inner journey." In his soul, Merton had already travelled East, before he went East with his feet, "seeking to become," he said, "as good a Buddhist as I can." When Merton went to Asia, he did not need to bring Christ with him, but sought to find him there. "The true missionary seeks Christ where he is going," said

Merton. And Merton, to make the point, noted how the great Jesuit missionary to China, Matteo Ricci, "divested himself of all that belonged to his own country and his own race and adapted all the good customs and attitudes of the land to which he had been gone." "In this," said Merton, "in this brief epiphany of the son of man, as a Chinese scholar, the 17th century Jesuit set an example to modern Christians of the kind of dialogue that must be established with the world's non-Christian religions."

Now does Merton mean these expressions literally? I mean, it's surely a kind of pious, Christian kindness to speak about this Hindu saviour, Christ is a Chinese scholar—but do we mean this literally? Does Merton mean it? Does he believe that the Christ might appear in our time in some Asian land—preaching a Confucian, familistic ethic, speaking of *yin* and *yang*—rather than the Greek *logos* and Western process philosophy? Did Merton really think that he could find Christ in Asia? In Ceylon, Merton saw some statutes of the Buddha, and about these he says, "I don't know when in my life I have ever had such a sense of beauty and of spiritual validity, running together in one aesthetic. This says everything, it needs nothing."

But what has happened to Jesus? What has happened to Christianity? Do we put these things down, these statements down, to Merton's ebullience and profusiveness in the moment where, surely, Buddhist now, Confucianist in the next moment, Trappist when he comes home, or did these have a meaning? No. I think Thomas Merton found Christ in Asia. Our Christian consolers assure us that Merton's interest in Eastern religions operated on the level of mutual cultural enrichment: as if superiority still in some way belonged to Christianity; as if Merton did not really seek to find Christ outside of Christianity. But that, I contend, is exactly what he did and what he was intending to do.

But it will be protested that Merton himself clearly states that Christianity, and only Christianity, is the supernaturally revealed religion, and surely he does. For example, he says, "Zen is not kerygma, but realization, not revelation, but consciousness." And he says, "First of all it is quite clear that no non-Christian religion or philosophy has anything that Christianity needs insofar as it is a supernaturally revealed religion."

Consider these statements. And you will see, in fact, the radical character of Merton's viewpoint. Zen, he says, "is not revelation, it's only realization." I mean, after all, you don't have the realization in Christianity, but we've got the revelation of it. Boy, listen to what he says: "non-Christian religion is not revelation, it's only the incarnation of Christ." Merton is saying, well, of course, supernaturally revealed religion, that's Christianity. Of course, kerygma, that's Christianity. Of course, all those things we learn in theological school, that's Christianity. But incarnation, realization—and I'm talking about the incarnation of Christ and the realization of Christ and the consciousness of Christ—well, those things you find in Asia.

What especially fascinated Merton about the East was its inveterate fondness for paradox. This intellectual and spiritual proclivity has been somehow lost in the West, and we are the poorer for it. Surely the Christian doctrine of the Incarnation—that God became enfleshed in Jesus Christ—is the consummate paradox. Yet the theologians of the West, with the exception of the mystical theologians, have often tried to circumscribe God with their logic. Such, for Merton, is the legacy of Descartes: the curse of an exaggerated rationalism. The East, on the other hand, has always suspected the untoward ways of reason, the tyranny of the ego and the disassembling ways of abstraction. Because of its preference for paradox and the intuitive method over the scientism of the West, Merton found a kindred spirit in Eastern monasticism. Paradoxically, it was a student of the East, the Venerable

Doctor Brahmachari, who had introduced Merton as a young university student to the spirituality of the West, particularly Saint Augustine and Thomas à Kempis.

Glenn Hinson addresses Merton's abiding interest in the non-Christian faiths of the East, reminding us that it predated his attraction to Catholicism:

> Before he converted to Catholicism, as is well known, he had a keen interest in Eastern religion, which, surprisingly, seemed to make him at times more appreciative of it than of Protestantism. During the '40s and '50s, it is true that he regularly criticized Eastern religion with the stock charge of pantheism, immanentism and absorptionism.
>
> In *The Seven Storey Mountain*, he concluded that Oriental mysticism, with which he had flirted in 1937 and 1938, belonged purely to the natural order. And while not per se evil, was more or less useless except when it is mixed up with elements that are strictly diabolical. He was, however, impressed with Brahmachari, who directed him to Augustine's *Confessions* and *The Imitation of Christ* and to a new Hindu religious order founded by him. In an essay written in 1961, entitled "Christian Culture Needs Oriental Wisdom," Merton wrote that Western society had a fatal flaw that the wisdom of the Orient might help to correct. He constructed an unequivocating *apologia* for the study of Eastern religions in the West.
>
> "The study of humanities in the West," he insisted, "absolutely must be introduced to the elements of contemplation, as well as wise action. This cannot be achieved simply by going back over European and Christian cultural traditions. We have to gain new perspectives, and on this our spiritual and even our physical survival may depend. This is not to suggest that Christianity is inherently deficient, rather it is to say that Christianity, if nothing else, can learn more about its own revelation by the

study of other religions. In the past it has been enriched by other traditions, for example Greek philosophy, Roman law, and Oriental philosophy and religious thought. Westerners can no longer afford to shrug off the Eastern faiths as pantheistic and quietistic."

He adopted the same stance towards these faiths as he did towards Protestantism or Orthodoxy. As a Catholic, he needed to acknowledge truth wherever he found it. Merton, for obvious reasons, felt the closest affinity with the monastic and contemplative traditions of other faiths. As most of us are aware, Merton felt very comfortable with Zen Buddhism.

The Asian Journal shows that he quaffed eagerly from the Buddhist cup in his journey to the East, always testing by the contemplative tradition he knew. He revelled in contact with the Dalai Lama, placing this above all his other experiences. What impressed him was their ability to communicate with one another and share an essentially spiritual experience of Buddhism, which is also somehow in harmony with Christianity, he said.

And in a November 7th entry he confessed that "in that depth, the spiritual experience he found among Buddhist monks, a deeper attainment and certitude than in Catholic contemplatives." Some persons, to be sure, feared he was going too far and questioned the viability of East–West dialogue. In Merton's case, however, I think that such fears failed to take into account the way in which he continually measured everything by Catholic tradition, especially the contemplative tradition. He put everything through a Catholic sieve to remove items that would not mix well with his own experience.

Certainly Merton demonstrated both originality and a critical ability to synthesize in his study of the common ground between Eastern and Western religious thought. He discovered in the writings of the Taoist sages and the

Buddhist mystics the wisdom of the Desert Fathers, the Rhine mystics of the 14th century, and William Blake. He found a necessary complement to the West's rationalism and empiricism in the naked vision and spiritual openness of the East. Herbert Richardson situates Merton's thinking within the context of contemporary debates around Christology, debates fraught with tension, canonical censures, pioneering insights, radical incursions into previously judged heterodox terrain, and various claims to a deeper fidelity. Catholic theologians and spiritual writers such as Elizabeth Johnson, Roger Haight, Michael Amaladoss, Jacques Dupuis, Tissa Balasuriya and Anthony De Mello have all experienced Roman discipline and the hierarchy's troubled incomprehension. Merton managed to avoid doctrinal confusion or the condemnation by ecclesiastical authorities of his theological and mystical probes by means of his untimely death. A rigorous scrutiny of his posthumously published *Asian Journal* would have landed him in serious hot water. But time and divinity intervened.

Richardson identifies some of the prophetic and "heretical" potentialities in Merton's last encounter with Eastern thought:

> Merton increasingly looked for the consciousness and the realization and the incarnation of the Christ in the East. It should be acknowledged that Merton's Christology is not typical of the Western Church. It is what scholars call Alexandrian, and of course that Christology we're always being told in the West, that Christology verges on the heretical because of its proclivity to see Christ in all things as the principle of universal divine participation in life. Consider, for example, this Christological statement, which is Merton's decisive and controlling affirmation in the final two pages of his *New Seeds of Contemplation*.

"For in becoming man, God became not only Jesus Christ but also potentially every man and woman that ever existed. In Christ, God became not only this man but also in a broader and mystical sense no less truly every man. Therefore there should be no one on earth in whom we are not prepared to see the presence of Christ, the presence of the Messiah."

And here now is Merton's harshest and hardest point for us who stand in the Christian tradition to hear. He says that we must go to other religions precisely because even though Christ is revealed in Christianity, Christ is incarnate and realized outside Christianity.

Hence, Merton had to leave the West in order to find Christ incarnate in Buddhism. The reason why Christ cannot be found incarnate in Christianity today is because—these are my theological reflections on Merton's argument—is because Christianity identifies the incarnation with only one person, Jesus. And from thence only one institution, the Church. And from thence to only one race, the "European Russian-American complex," Merton's words, which we call the West, "whose sin," he says, "is its unmitigated arrogance towards the human race. But," Merton continues, "since the Word was made flesh, God is in all of us and all of us are to be seen and treated as Christ." I might say that in my reading of Christian theology and of Merton, it is *Merton* who is Orthodox.

William Nicholls sees a new and different Merton in the East, but one continuous with his past—a natural evolution and maturation of spiritual consciousness:

We find him in so many expected and unexpected meetings— sharing a whiskey in the airport bar with the American wife on the way to join her husband in Viet Nam; so delightfully taken with the Jain lady with the big brown eyes and the white sari he met at the interreligious conference; sharing spiritual experience and insight with Rinpoches in the Himalayas; and an audience with the Dalai Lama himself.

Because he is with himself, he can be all these people. He need not fear impurity with his encounters with women. He does not feel superior or inferior to those great representatives with another religion. He is present to each.

The photographs of Merton reproduced in the *Asian Journal* make an interesting comparison with some of even the best of the Gethsemani pictures of the early monastic years. A new Merton is revealed in these last photographs; he looks healthy for the first time almost since his youth, happy and fulfilled—a man among men. This Merton who can eat and drink, as well as think, wait and fast is probably something of a scandal to the pious. One is reminded of the reaction of the disciples of Buddha when he abandoned asceticism and took enough nourishment to give him health and strength for his meditation. Merton looks real, authentic, fulfilled.

He needed to get away from Gethsemani, he says in *The Asian Journal*. Perhaps he also needed to grow beyond the monastic identity. Even the new hermitage, which gave him so much more chance to be himself, was perhaps now a constriction to the extent that it could be regarded as the answer—the answer was within himself from other people, not in a particular identity or special way of life. There is some evidence that in these last months he was discovering this genuine answer. He even began to move beyond the monastic and religious identity, not by denying it but by transcending it. The happy and fulfilled human maturity so evident in *The Asian Journal* was the outcome of an inner journey now nearing its goal.

The final doctrine can be as well expressed in Zen as in Christian and Catholic terms, as Merton himself was well able to show on the basis of the historical scholarship at his command. But the particular edge that Merton gives to the concepts is really only explicable in the light of his dialogue with Zen and his awareness of the contemporary developments in psychology.

As Merton writes:

Zen implies a breakthrough, an explosive liberation from one dimensional conformism; a recovery of unity which is not the suppression of opposites but the simplicity beyond opposites. To exist and function in the world of opposites while experiencing that world in terms of a primal simplicity does imply, if not a formal metaphysic, at least a ground of metaphysical intuition. This means a totally different perspective than that which dominates our society and enables it to dominate us. Hence the Zen saying 'before I grasped Zen the mountains were nothing but mountains and rivers nothing but rivers. When I got into Zen the mountains were no longer mountains and the rivers no longer rivers. But when I understood Zen the mountains were only mountains and the rivers only rivers.' The point is that facts are not just plain facts; there is a dimension where the bottom drops out of the world of factuality and of the ordinary.

Western industrial culture is in the curious position of having simultaneously reached the climax of an entire totalitarian rationality of organization and of complete absurdity and self-contradiction. Existentialists and a few others have noticed the absurdity but the majority persists in seeing only the rational machinery against which no protest avails because, after all, it is rational and it is a fact. So too is the internal contradiction. The thing about Zen is that it pushes contradictions to their ultimate limits, where one has to choose between madness and innocence. And Zen suggests that we may be driving towards one or the other on a cosmic scale; driving towards them because one way or the other as madmen or innocents we are already there. It might be good to open our eyes and see.

On his Asian journey we notice a radiant, healthy and intel-
lectually vivacious Merton, a man looking for knowledge,
armed with empathy and curiosity. Talking about the Asian
trip, co-traveller Amiya Chakravarty tenderly observed:

> On an impulse I asked him, do you have an hour or so to spare
> today? I want to take you to an artist's home. I think you will
> understand each other. Immediately he said, I can go now. So
> along with Professor Naresh Guha, we went to Jamini Roy, one
> of the most revered painters of modern India. White-haired and
> radiant, this artist met us at the door and took us to his studio
> rooms, where Indian life painted in colour and in black-and-
> white etchings stood still and beautiful on the walls.
>
> The range and depth of his art was overpowering, and
> yet made one feel strangely at home in this assured tranquil-
> ity. "Tell the American saint," said Jamini Roy, "that this is my
> avocation, my life. I live here with my family and myself, prepare
> the colours, the paper and the brushes. My life is one." Merton
> replied, "As a Trappist monk, my life, too, is one piece in the way
> you have put it. If I make cheese, it has to be right. If I work on
> the land, I draw a straight furrow. If I sing the Gregorian chant,
> it has to be authentic." This oneness and depth and simplicity
> brought the two men together.
>
> We walked together until Merton stopped in front of a
> picture of Christ. It was done in an early Syriac style. Jamini
> Roy had never been in the West. And his own traditions were
> different. But he had drawn upon some deep moment of affinity
> and devotion. The blue infinitude, the crucifixion, the glory and
> the total gift to humanity were there. This picture I decided to
> acquire for Thomas Merton.
>
> I asked him whether I should take it to his monastery
> in Gethsemani on his return. He paused and said there is a
> convent in the Redwood area in California where a few nuns live

in prayer, poverty and beatitude. They would treasure it. I did take this picture to Mother Miriam the Abbess of the Redwood Convent after I had recovered from the shock of Thomas Merton's sudden passing. And I remember how in the pure air of the convent, with great trees watching and the blue Pacific stretching from the valley below, nuns gathered around the picture. They felt as Merton did.

Having finally arrived at Bangkok, Thailand, Merton lived out the final hours of his life. John Howard Griffin comments on Merton's last day and the circumstances of his death:

When he got to Bangkok, he gave his talk on the morning of the tenth, the anniversary of his entry into the monastery. And he was very tired; the heat was oppressive and he hadn't had a nap the day before. So since he was going to have to answer the questions in the evening, he went to his cabin and took a shower and he was never really a practical man about things. He put on a pair of shorts or short pajamas and barefoot and still damp walked across the terrazzo floor and, they had these very tall fans, and he reached for the fan to turn it on to the pallet where he was going to take his nap on the floor. It was DC current and it went into him and he was staying in a cabin with three other people but it wasn't till about an hour later that they went and the door was locked from the inside, it was a double kind of a door with a little curtain on the upper part, and they saw him, lying on the floor on his back with this big fan cross-wise across his body.

The blades had stopped rotating but the current was still alive and it was still burning. He was very deeply burnt in that angle across the body. There was a Benedictine Nun Superior from Korea at that meeting, who, before she became religious, was an Austrian physician and a specialist in internal medicine and a very, very fine one. Word spread immediately, so she came immediately, thinking she might be of some help. He was already dead, but she gave him an immediate examination. And she determined he died from the effects of electric shock.

Herbert Richardson found a special meaning in Merton's bizarre Asian death:

> Thomas Merton's Asian death is God's lifting up his special meaning for us. Arriving home there in Bangkok, his life found its consummation in what Benedictine monk Aldhelm Cameron-Brown calls a type of Zen death. This occurs, says Cameron-Brown, when a man stays in one monastery for over 25 years, hardly ever leaving it except to go to a nearby town, and then at last travels halfway around the world to die suddenly on foreign soil.
>
> "Merton," Cameron-Brown says, "would have laughed at the absurdity of such a death." But shall we? Is the form, the place and time of Merton's death meaningless? Or is it, within that providence which leads us, God's way of permanently fixing Merton in Asia so that we who love him must seek him there? God has made his pilgrimage, I suggest, a pioneering for us, a mediation of the East to the West.

Merton's efforts at interreligious mediation are without parallel. He found a theological modality that balanced the contraries, achieved a creative harmony among competing systems of belief, stripped creeds of their Urizenic control, and freed the spirit to soar, not by means of a superficial capitulation to trendy efforts that lead to a false ecumenicity, but by means of a contemplative co-sympathy that rattles the spiritual and intellectual complacency of atrophied structures. As the Olivetan Benedictine monk Laurence Freeman says, "If a tradition does not change us and the way we live each new day, it has become sclerotic, a mere ideology, a knot of opinions."

Merton knew that the revivifying springs of authentic contemplation can nurture a deepening dialogue among faiths, and his own numerous encounters with other religious traditions provide a model for our current struggles to make sense of religious pluralism, to value religious diversity, and yet to seek new commonalities. Merton scholar Joseph Raab rightly situates the monk of Gethsemani's evolving understanding of and respect for meaningful and substantive interfaith dialogue in the context of his personal spiritual history, innovative strategies and heroic fidelity to his own tradition:

> Catholics and other Christians interested in resolving the tension, which sometimes becomes a contradiction, between openness and fidelity to one's own faith would do well to follow Merton's example. As the "rip-roaring Trappist" of *The Seven Storey Mountain* gradually matured, he began to be open to the wisdom of other contemplative traditions.
>
> As a young monk, he was often concerned to assure himself of his orthodoxy by offering merely pejorative accounts of any tradition other than Catholic. Thomas Merton, however, eventually learned to understand others by allowing them to speak for themselves, without first imposing his own categories upon their language.
>
> But even the elder Merton would try to integrate his newly acquired understandings within the framework of his own religious faith. He had little choice, really, taking the final step. Merton's mind was habitually moving toward higher forms of synthesis; he was always striving for a further horizon capable of integrating seemingly opposing and disparate views, if at all possible.

6

Icon of Wholeness

WILLIAM BLAKE, JOHN Cassian, the Desert Fathers, the English paradise mystics and Thomas Aquinas opened Merton to a prophetic contemplation; his affective connection with the wisdom of the East ensured that contradictions will be subsumed into a higher mystery and that an encompassing unity awaits all who yearn to know the Holy.

In the end, like all great pilgrims in search of the place they have left in order to know it for the first time, Merton returned to his Kentucky monastery to be buried. Amiya Chakravarty reminisced about his last farewell:

> I decided once more to go to Gethsemani, which I did. This is some time after his body was flown over. While walking in the garden, Brother Patrick Hart suddenly showed me a little black cross in that garden that was all there was to commemorate Thomas Merton. He didn't want an elaborate grave or symbols of holiness or special power. That marvellous little cross that moved one more deeply than one can imagine. All of that life was consecrated in that tiny mound with that tiny black cross. As I walked back from the monastery, the little cross that I had seen, he was there in the world in which we live. He was also somewhere in a realm that most of us cannot reach.

I felt once more the utter tenderness, the infinitude of a life lived with courage and an encompassing wholeness—these are my devoted memories of Thomas Merton, whose redemptive holiness is a light to all of us who knew him and will continue to shine in the hearts of people who will know him as the ages pass.

Acknowledgements

THE GENESIS OF this book can be found in the confluence of two directly connected but somewhat serendipitously conceived and orchestrated events: the first international symposium on the life and thought of Thomas Merton, convened at the Vancouver School of Theology at the University of British Columbia in May of 1978, and then the creation of the CBC *Ideas* series "Thomas Merton: Extraordinary Man," based in great measure on the scholarship, the voices and the energy of the symposium. The series was initially aired in December of the same year, the tenth anniversary of Merton's death in Bangkok, Thailand.

Although *The Unquiet Monk: Thomas Merton's Questing Faith* is structured along the lines of the CBC series and draws significantly from the hitherto unpublished proceedings and interviews that are the heart of the program, it is augmented with subsequent research and several decades of Merton scholarship, including the collection of essays by several Merton friends and scholars, *Thomas Merton: Pilgrim in Process.*

I am particularly indebted to the abiding commitment, labour and learning of my original colleague and partner at the VST/UBC symposium: Rev. Dr. Donald Grayston; to the original cast of producers involved in the creation of the CBC series: Geraldine Sherman, Len Scher and Jill Eisen; to the many scholars who appear in the book and who were the foundation stone at the symposium; to my spouse and life partner, Krystyna, who has reliably assisted with numerous Merton conferences, books and documentaries over the years with admirable critical insight; and to St. Jerome's University in the University of Waterloo, Ontario, which has been the driving and organizing force for numerous international and national conferences and study days on the work of Thomas Merton and that houses in its archives the best of Canadian scholarship on the Merton legacy.